More
Specialities of the House

collected by
Kathy Eldon

Assistant Editor: Phoebe Vreeland
Cover painting: Phyllis Thomas

Dedicated to Alan Bobbe, with
great admiration
and to Mike, Dan and Amy
with love

First published in 1989 by
Kenway Publications Ltd
P.O. Box 18800
Nairobi, Kenya

Graphics and Phototypesetting by
Kul Graphics Ltd, Box 18095, Funzi Road, Nairobi, Kenya

Printed by
General Printers Ltd, P.O. Box 18001, Homa Bay Road, Nairobi, Kenya

ISBN 9966 - 848 - 11 - 8

Contents

Contents

Three years ago I had the rather cheeky idea of squeezing some highly guarded secrets from a group of Kenyan chefs. To my surprise, they appeared only too delighted to spill the beans, and gave me their favourite recipes. To everyone's delight, the first edition of **Specialities of the House** sold out within a few months and has been reprinted for an enthusiastic audience. There are obviously many people who are pleased to have the opportunity to recreate the specialities of Kenya's favourite restaurants at home.

Despite this competition, the restaurants whose recipes were featured have stayed in business. Perhaps encouraged by the maxim that imitation is the sincerest form of flattery, Kenya's chefs have responded equally enthusiastically to my new efforts to expose their innermost secrets. This new collection of recipes represents an even broader look at the restaurants, and includes such diverse cuisine as French, Japanese, Swahili—even Yugoslav! There are popular hors d'oeuvres, main courses, desserts and drinks in this new, very special collection. Try the recipes at home knowing that although the food may reproduce, you will never be able to recreate the unique ambience of the great restaurants in Kenya.

Once again, I salute the generous chefs who have shared their secrets with us.

Kathy Eldon

Aberdare Country Club

The attractions of the Aberdare Country Club are myriad. First of all there is the air. Crisp and perfectly clear, it stimulates the senses and focuses your attention on the superb view: strutting peacocks in the foreground, a vision of green forests and a dramatic sky behind. Then you move inside. The lounge of the former farmhouse is dominated by a massive stone fireplace where logs burn nightly, while in the rambling dining rooms home-cooked meals are served. The food is the creation of Vena Johannson, who has made the buffet lunches world famous. I still dream about Vena's chilli butter, a regular accompaniment to her lavish Sunday curry lunches, and I am tortured by the memory of her flaky Napoleon pastries and yummy puddings. Vena is a quiet, under-stated cooking genius, who deserves a cookbook all to herself. She has graciously shared some of her simpler recipes, all of which make use of Kenya's outstanding fruits and vegetables, rich dairy products and ocean catch.

Cocktail Ananas   vodka-soaked pineapple with mint

Smoked Sailfish Paté   a uniquely Kenyan starter

Muesli   healthy breakfast fare

Banana Bread   a versatile bread

Mushroom and Bean Salad   yoghurty vegetables

Vena's Ice Cream   infinitely variable ice cream

Cocktail Ananas
Refreshing way to start or end a meal

4 slices fresh pineapple
2 tablespoons chopped mint leaves
4 tablespoons Kenya Cane or vodka
4 sprigs mint leaves
2 cocktail cherries, halved

Chop pineapple into neat cubes and place in a bowl. Add chopped mint and vodka. Chill. Just before serving frost cocktail glasses with pale green sugar (add green food colouring to sugar in a plastic bag and shake). Fill glasses with pineapple. Decorate with sprigs of mint and cherries.

Serves 4

Smoked Sailfish Paté
Serve with melba toast and butter

250 g (8oz) smoked sailfish or tuna pieces
125 g (1½ cups) fresh breadcrumbs
grated rind of lemon or lime
3 tablespoons lime or lemon juice
ground black pepper
3-4 cloves garlic, crushed
3 teaspoons finely chopped onion
60 g (¼ cup) melted butter
125 ml (½ cup) cream
chopped parsley for garnish

Mince, blend, or finely chop the fish. Add breadcrumbs, lemon rind and juice, onions, garlic and pepper. Add cream and butter to make a soft consistency. Divide and serve on lettuce leaves. Pass around fresh melba toast or brown bread and butter.

Serves 4

Muesli

This keeps well in an airtight container

4 cups porridge oats
½ cup brown sugar
½ cup wheat germ
½ cup desiccated coconut
½ cup All Bran, or other bran cereal
1 cup chopped nuts
½ cup honey
½ cup oil
dried fruit (optional)

Mix dry ingredients together. Pour oil and honey over mixture. Mix thoroughly. Spread in roasting pan and place in oven (Gas Mark 4, 180°C, 350°F) for 25 minutes or until toasted. Stir occasionally to prevent sticking. Serve cold with milk or yoghurt and fresh fruit.

Makes 8 cups

Banana Bread

Serve hot for tea or toasted with cream cheese for breakfast

250 g (2 cups) plain flour
115 g (½ cup) sugar
60 g (4 tablespoons) margarine
1 level teaspoon baking powder
½ teaspoon baking soda
3 large ripe bananas, mashed
milk
½ cup chopped nuts (optional)

Sift flour, baking powder and baking soda. Rub in margarine until well blended. Stir in mashed bananas and enough milk to give a soft dropping consistency. Stir in nuts if desired. Pour into a greased loaf tin and bake in a moderate oven (Gas Mark 4, 180°C, 350°F) for 30 minutes, then reduce the temperature (Gas Mark 3, 170°C, 325°F) for about another 45 minutes until well risen and firm to the touch in the centre.

Makes one loaf

Mushroom and Bean Salad
A fresh way to serve Kenya's fine produce

250 g (2 cups) mushrooms
1½ cups fresh green beans
250 ml (1 cup) yoghurt
1 teaspoon sugar
1 clove garlic, crushed
salt and pepper to taste

Wash the mushrooms and drain well. Chop, removing tougher stems. Trim, de-thread and cut the beans into bite-size pieces. Blanch the beans for 5 minutes. Refresh under cold water. When cool mix all ingredients thoroughly and chill before serving.

Serves 6

Vena's Ice Cream
Rum or chocolate can be substituted for vanilla

1 litre (4 cups) double cream
3 eggs
1 500 ml (14 oz) tin condensed milk
1 teaspoon vanilla essence

Beat cream until thick. Separate eggs. Whip egg yolks until light. Add vanilla and condensed milk. Beat until blended. Combine cream and milk mixtures. Whip egg whites until stiff. Fold into mixture. Freeze.

Serves 10

Akasaka

Highly polished dark wooden tables and simple paper walls provide clean lines and an air of serenity for the Akasaka, Nairobi's first and most popular Japanese restaurant. The owner, Mr Ichiro Hirai, is a gracious host and a good ambassador for Japan. Most of his customers are old regulars who like the unique blend of flavours, textures and colours created by the Kenyan chefs. I enjoy eating in the simply furnished private dining room, where patrons sit, shoeless, backs supported, at a low table and try to eat with chopsticks. Friendly waitresses serve the food in the traditional Japanese style, kneeling by the table to prepare sukiyaki on electric hot plates. Somehow the food tastes better with the extra ritual.

Miso Soup   you need "miso" or soybean paste to prepare this traditional soup

Grilled Aubergines   a simple, attractive starter

Yakitori   gingery barbecued chicken

Beef Sukiyaki   quickly fried beef with vegetables

Seafood Tempura   delicately battered deep-fried seafood with simple sauces

Miso Soup
Vary by adding sliced fresh mushrooms or tinned Japanese mushrooms

1 litre (4 cups) clear soup stock or water
1 small carrot, grated
1 small onion, diced
100 g (4 oz) miso (soybean paste)
175 g (6 oz) tofu cut into 2.5 cm (1 inch)
  squares
1 pinch togarashi (black and/or hot
  pepper can be used as substitute)
1 spring onion for garnish

Combine stock, carrot and onion and bring to a boil. Then reduce the heat and simmer for 5 minutes. Remove 1 cup liquid. Add miso and stir to creamy paste. Return paste to pan and stir. Drop in tofu. Return to boil. Turn off heat, add pinch of togarashi and stir. Serve immediately in small bowls garnished with chopped spring onion.

Serves 4

Grilled Aubergines
Use a charcoal fire if possible

450 g (1 lb) aubergines, halved
salt
soy sauce
sugar

Prepare aubergines by salting heavily. Turn upside down on a draining rack and allow bitter juices to drain. Rinse thoroughly and dry well. Preheat grill (oven grill is fine as a substitute). Lightly salt, and baste with soy sauce and a sprinkle of sugar. Grill until soft, but cooked through, about 2-3 minutes.

Serves 4

Yakitori
Thread small pieces of chicken on to metal or bamboo skewers

2 chicken breasts, boned
3 tablespoons soy sauce
2 tablespoons sugar
1 teaspoon powdered ginger
1 clove garlic, crushed
1 teaspoon oil
1 tablespoon toasted sesame seeds

Cut chicken into small pieces. In a small saucepan combine other ingredients, except oil and sesame seeds. Bring to boil. Remove from heat and cool. Place chicken in the mixture and marinate for 30 minutes. Oil skewers. Thread chicken on. Grill over high heat (or under oven broiler) for 6-8 minutes, turning over once or twice and brushing with marinade. Serve well browned. Moisten with remaining marinade and sprinkle with toasted sesame seeds.

Serves 4 as a starter

Beef Sukiyaki
Can be attractively prepared at the table

125 ml (½ cup) soy sauce
250 ml (1 cup) water or soup stock
3 tablespoons sugar
2 tablespoons sweet sherry
450 g (1 lb) lean beef fillet steak,
   thinly sliced
1 large onion, halved and sliced
6 spring onions, chopped
225 g (8 oz) mushrooms, sliced thinly

Combine first four ingredients. Mix well, pour into jug. Arrange remaining ingredients, except oil, on large serving dishes and place on table next to hot plate. Seat guests. Heat a large frying pan on hot plate and add oil. When very hot, add half the beef and fry until just brown on both sides. Push beef to one side. Drop in half the onions and fry lightly. Add half the mushrooms and cabbage, keeping separate. Add half the sauce and cook for 3-4 minutes. Add some tofu and spinach and cook another 3-4 minutes. Each guest should break an egg into a small bowl and beat lightly with chopsticks. Guests may help themselves to the

225 g (8 oz) spinach, coarsely chopped
225 g (8 oz) Chinese, or other white
    cabbage chopped into 1.25 cm
    (½ inch) strips
175 g (6 oz) tofu, cut into 2.5 cm
    (1 inch) squares (optional)
4 tablespoons oil
4 eggs

cooked meat and vegetables. Traditionally beef is dipped in raw egg before eating. As pan is emptied, add more ingredients and keep cooking till all is cooked.

Serves 4

Tempura
Quick frying in hot oil ensures the delicacy of this dish

For each person: about 350 g (12 oz) of any vegetables you wish such as artichoke hearts, broccoli, carrots, aubergines, cauliflower, green beans, mushrooms, pumpkin, sweet potatoes, green peppers—at room temperature
For each person: the same quantity of seafood, such as chunks of fish, prawns, lobster, mussels
For 4 persons:
100 g (¾ cup) plain flour
1 egg
275 ml (1 cup and 2 tablespoons) water
oil for frying

Prepare vegetables by cutting in bite-sized pieces or strips. Prepare seafood in the same fashion, removing all shells, and cutting fish into chunks. Combine rest of ingredients together and whisk lightly. Do not stir again once batter is mixed. Pour 5-7.5 cm (2-3 inches) oil in a deep frying pan. Heat to 175°C (320-350°F) and maintain at this temperature. (A small blob of batter will turn golden brown at this temperature.) Use chopsticks or tongs to dip pieces of vegetables or seafood into batter. Shake off excess and drop coated food into oil. Fry only a few at once, leaving strong tasting foods till last. Allow to crisp and brown, turning as necessary. Remove from oil and drain on absorbent paper. Transfer to a warm oven. Remove floating bits with a slotted spoon and fry another portion. Take care to keep oil hot. Serve immediately with Tempura Sauce.

Tempura Sauce (Tentsuyu)

Prepare before frying tempura

250 ml (1 cup) soup stock or water
50 ml (2 tablespoons) soy sauce
50 ml (2 tablespoons) sweet sherry
100 g (4 oz) daikon (white raddish),
   grated
50 g (2 oz) fresh ginger root, grated

Combine stock, soy sauce and sherry and bring to boil. Cool and divide among four bowls. Add a portion of daikon and ginger to each.

Serves 4

Alan Bobbe's guest book reads like a "Who's Who" of anyone who is anyone and has visited Kenya. Film stars like Sydney Poitier, Bing Crosby and Robert Redford and film director Sydney Pollack have all stopped in for a meal, along with assorted archdukes and duchesses, famous food writers and any tourist who has ever read a guide to Kenya. Alan treats them all alike, with a sense of mischief and a naughty joke if he's in the mood. His food has always been light and beautiful—long before anyone had ever heard of Nouvelle Cuisine. It arrives piping hot, served, if you're lucky, by the wittiest headwaiters in the country, Michael and Joseph. I am full of admiration for the whole crowd—and have dedicated this second collection of the finest recipes in the land to the greatest chef of them all, Alan Bobbe!

Soup a l'oignon   rich and cheesy

Truite en Chemise   trout in a nightgown!

Alan Bobbe's Crepes   your guests will swoon

Kongo Kuku   chicken, peanuts and green peppers—Africa   style

Beans Provencale   tender green beans with anchovies and capers

Forgotten Bananas   a chic and easy dessert

Soup a l'oignon
Serve with a glass of red wine for a light meal

4 onions, thinly sliced
30 g (2 tablespoons) butter
1 teaspoon sugar
1.5 litres (6 cups) boiling water
salt and pepper to taste
225 g (8 oz) bread, cut into 1.5·cm
   (½ inch) slices
4 slices cheese
60 ml (4 tablespoons) melted butter
30 ml (2 tablespoons) red wine

In Alan Bobbe's words, "this soup is simple to make: all it requires is kindness and respect". Brown onions in butter over low heat, stirring with a wooden spoon. In 20 minutes sprinkle sugar over onions and add boiling water, salt and pepper. Boil covered for 10 minutes. Place cut bread in a fireproof dish or casserole. Cover each slice of bread with very thin slices of cheese. Pour over the contents of the saucepan. Sprinkle melted butter on top. Place casserole in a moderate oven (Gas Mark 4, 180°C, 350°F) for about 20 minutes. Before serving, sprinkle with a drop of red wine.

Serves 4

Truite en Chemise
Light crepes are the secret of this delicate, but easy dish

4 trout, about 225 g (8 oz) each
1½ cups finely chopped mushrooms
4 tablespoons cream
90 ml (1/3 cup) lemon juice
salt and freshly ground black pepper
200 g (¾ cup) butter

Alan thanks the Tamarind Group in Nairobi for the fact that we are able to purchase fresh trout which have never been introduced to a deep freezer, which makes all the difference in the world to the delicate taste of this sublime fish. He slits each trout down the belly, washes and dries it and stuffs it with as many chopped mushrooms as it will hold. Moisten with cream, lemon juice and seasonings. Skewer opening together. Melt butter in an oven-proof dish and bake in hot oven (Gas Mark 6, 200°C, 400°F), for 15 minutes, basting three or four times during cooking. The fish should be cooked through but not browned. Remove from oven and drain. Roll in a crepe, folding sides of crepe in. Serve immediately. See following recipe for crepes.

Serves 4

Alan Bobbe's Crepes
If you don't wish to use kirsch and rum, substitute water

250 g (2 cups) flour, sifted
5 slightly beaten eggs
60 ml (¼ cup) lukewarm water
60 ml (¼ cup) beer
1 tablespoon rum
1 tablespoon kirsch
¼ teaspoon salt

Place flour in a bowl. Stir in eggs and remaining ingredients. Whisk till absolutely smooth and put aside for 4 hours. Alan says this recipe is very exotic and when you serve it with the trout your guests will offer you the earth for the recipe or else swoon at your feet!

Makes 10

Kongo Kuku
Serve this uniquely flavoured chicken with white rice

1½ kg (3 lb) chicken
125 g (½ cup) butter
handful of peanuts
salt to taste
6 green peppers
1 tablespoon oil
4 tablespoons or more peanut butter
1 cup unsalted roasted peanuts,
    chopped or coarsely ground

Wash the chicken inside and prepare for roasting by packing with butter and a handful of peanuts. Rub chicken with salt and dabs of butter. Roast in moderate oven (Gas Mark 4, 180°C, 350°F), about 20 minutes to the pound. Now heat a tablespoon of oil in a frying pan. Cook whole green peppers over high heat, turning often until blackened outside. Cool, cut off tops and scoop out seeds. Cut flesh into strips and put in the oven around the chicken. Baste with the melted butter from the pan. When chicken is tender, spread with peanut butter and salt. Sprinkle a cup of chopped peanuts over chicken. Return to oven and cook another 5-6 minutes. Serve surrounded by green peppers.

Serves 4

Beans Provençale
Use the tiniest Kenyan beans available

4 cups French green beans
salt and pepper
3 tablespoons olive oil
¼ cup capers
2 tins anchovies
1 clove garlic, crushed
chopped parsley to garnish
chopped spring onions to garnish

Bring 2 cups water to boil in a saucepan. Add salt and pepper. Add cleaned beans and boil until just tender. Drain. Heat olive oil in a frying pan. Add capers, anchovies, garlic and beans. Toss until well mixed. Serve hot, garnished with parsley and chopped spring onions.

Serves 4-6

Forgotten Bananas
Alan inadvertently stumbled upon this unforgettable dessert

2 bananas per person
lime juice
brown sugar as desired

Peel bananas and split them lengthwise. Place in an ovenproof dish. Squeeze lime juice over bananas and dust with brown sugar. Bake in a moderate oven (Gas Mark 4, 180°C, 350°F) for 25-30 minutes until they puff up into a kind of purée/soufflé. Serve with a sauce made from bitter, chunky marmalade heated with a few tots of dark rum, a little lemon juice and brown sugar. It's a dessert fit for Alan Bobbe's Bistro.

Amboseli Grill

Pleasing tourists from around the world is not an easy task. But the Hilton has found a formula which combines the best of Kenyan ingredients and ideas with diverse influences, resulting in original food with a strong local flair. Expatriate chefs work closely with Kenyans, experimenting with traditional dishes to introduce tourists to something uniquely Kenyan. Superb presentation is always a prerequisite at the Amboseli Grill, perhaps best known for its extensive lunchtime buffet of delicious cold and hot selections and inviting desserts.

Fillet of Red Snapper with Garden Vegetables fish poached in a delicate sauce with tender garden vegetables

Chocolate Pavé with Mint Sauce dense chocolate in a pool of mint sauce

Fillet of Red Snapper with Garden Vegetables
Prepare a flavourful vegetable stock first

900 g (2 lb) fresh red snapper fillet
30 g (2 tablespoons) butter
2 cloves garlic, crushed
80 g (3 oz) shallots, sliced
400 ml (1½ cups) vegetable stock (made
  from leeks, onions, carrots,
  turnips, parsley and seasoned with black
  pepper corns, bay leaf and thyme)
1 litre (4 cups) fresh cream
40 ml (2 tablespoons) white wine
120 g (4 oz) carrots, cleaned, peeled
  and julienned
120 g (4 oz) fresh peas
120 g (4 oz) tomatoes, skinned, seeded and
  chopped
120 g (4 oz) turnips, cleaned, peeled
  and julienned
2 bunches fresh basil, chopped
lemon juice
salt and pepper to taste

Melt butter in a saucepan and sauté the shallots and garlic till tender. Arrange the fish fillets in the saucepan. Add vegetable stock, cream and wine. Place in a moderate oven (Gas Mark 4, 180°C, 350°F) for 15 minutes or until the fillets are just cooked. Meanwhile blanch the vegetables. When the fillets are cooked set aside in a warm oven and reduce the stock to a thick consistency. Add the blanched vegetables and simmer for a few minutes. Add chopped fresh basil. Add a few drops of lemon juice and correct seasonings. To serve make a bed of vegetables and sauce on a warmed plate and place the fillets on top.

Serves 6

Chocolate Pavé with Mint Sauce
Sinfully satisfying

300 g (10 oz) bittersweet chocolate
15 g (1 tablespoon) unsalted butter
4 tablespoons heavy cream
5 egg yolks, beaten
4 egg whites, beaten to form stiff peaks
1 litre (4 cups) heavy cream or milk
1 vanilla bean or 3 teaspoons vanilla
   extract
10 egg yolks
250 g (1 cup) sugar
mint extract to taste
cocoa powder
a few fresh mint leaves
fresh raspberries for garnish

To prepare the pavé melt the chocolate and butter in a double boiler. Over a very low heat add heavy cream and then the beaten egg yolks. Remove from heat and fold in stiff egg whites. Pour into a rectangular mould, about 2.5-5 cm (1-2 inches) deep, and refrigerate. To prepare the mint sauce bring cream (or milk) and vanilla nearly to a boil. In a bowl beat the egg yolks and sugar and add to the cream. Heat the mixture carefully for 5 minutes, but do not allow to boil or sauce will separate. Remove from heat and add mint extract. Allow to cool. Serve a slice of the pavé on a pool of mint sauce. Sprinkle with cocoa powder and decorate with mint leaves and berries.

Serves 6

The Bay Leaf is not a restaurant but a moveable feast which manages to satisfy the demanding palates and appetites of large numbers of Nairobi residents, turning out lovely creations from their modest catering kitchen. Stan and Annette Thomas are the brains behind the firm, which has been in the catering business since 1968. They can provide everything, from nourishing, sensible school lunches to the latest nouvelle cuisine delicacies for embassy parties. Blessed with great energy and determination, the Thomases enjoy adapting international cuisine to the strictures of Kenya, and have devised a variety of tasty recipes which are easy enough for novice cooks to prepare.

Cheesy Nutters   irresistible cocktail canapés
Ratatouille   summer vegetables in a French manner
Mangetout with Sesame Seeds   snowpeas with an oriental flavour

Tarte Tartin   caramelised fruit with crisp pastry
Kenyan Pawpaw Cake   a delightful dessert using local ingredients

Cheesy Nutters
Tasty accompaniment to a bowl of soup or glass of wine

125 g (1 cup) self-raising flour (or
   1 cup flour and 3 teaspoons baking
   powder)
40 g (¼ cup) maize meal (or ground rice)
1 teaspoon dry mustard
1 teaspoon curry powder
ground black pepper
125 g (½ cup) butter or margarine
75 g (1 cup) strong cheese, grated
20 macadamia nuts, neatly halved

Sieve the flour, maize meal and spices together. Cream the margarine. Add the grated cheese and work in the flour mixture. Form into approximately 40 small balls. Place on a large baking sheet, flatten slightly with a knife and press a half macadamia nut into the centre of each. Bake for 15-20 minutes (Gas Mark 4, 180°C, 350°F). Lift off with a spatula onto a cooling rack. Store in an air-tight tin.

Makes about 40

Ratatouille
Delicious hot or cold

2 tablespoons oil
2 onions, sliced
4 tomatoes, skinned, seeded and
   chopped
4 zucchini, sliced
4 aubergines, peeled, sliced and quartered
2 bell peppers (red and/or green), chopped
bouquet garni (thyme, bay leaf and
   parsley tied together)
2 cloves garlic
salt and black pepper

Heat oil in a non-stick pan and brown the onions. Add the vegetables, garlic and bouquet garni. Season with salt and pepper and allow to simmer uncovered for 30 minutes or until the juices have completely evaporated. Serve as a starter with pieces of French bread or as a main course. Left-over ratatouille makes a delicious filling for omelettes.

Serves 6

Mangetout with Sesame Seeds
An interesting way to serve this delicate vegetable

500 g mangetout (snow peas)
1 tablespoon sesame seeds
1 large clove garlic, crushed
2 tablespoons soy sauce

Put the sesame seeds on a baking tray and toast for 5 minutes in a medium oven (Gas Mark 4, 180°C, 350°F), shaking them from time to time. Trim the ends of the snow peas and steam them over simmering water until they are cooked but still crunchy. Mix the garlic and soy sauce and toss with the steamed peas mixing well. Sprinkle with toasted sesame seeds just before serving.

Serves 4

Tarte Tartin
a Kenyan adaptation of a classic French dessert

185 g (1½ cups) self-raising flour (or
   1½ cups flour plus 3 teaspoons   baking
powder)
4 teaspoons icing sugar
125 g (½ cup) unsalted butter
1 egg beaten with 1 tablespoon cold water
30 g (2 tablespoons) unsalted butter
150 g (2/3 cup) sugar
5 large dessert apples or pears or 1 small
   pineapple

Sieve flour and icing sugar into a bowl. Rub in butter until mixture looks like fine breadcrumbs. Make a well in the centre and use a spatula to stir in the egg mixture until the dough begins to form small lumps, then gently knead by hand. Set aside for 1 hour. To make filling: melt butter and sugar in a heavy pan over low heat until they caramelise. Pour into a 22.5 cm (9 inch) diameter shallow round tin. Peel, core and slice apples or pears into a bowl of water acidulated with lemon juice, or peel and cut pineapple in half, and remove the core. Slice into crescent shaped slices. Arrange fruit in overlapping circles over caramel. Roll out pastry to a 22.5 cm (9 inch) circle to fit just inside the tin, covering the fruit. Bake in

squeeze of lemon juice
1 cup heavy cream (optional)

a pre-heated oven (Gas mark 7, 220°C, 425°F) for 45 minutes. If after 20 minutes the pastry is getting too brown, reduce the temperature slightly and cover with a piece of greaseproof paper, but remember pastry should be brown and crisp. Place a serving dish over the finished tarte and invert while hot. Serve with fresh cream.

Serves 6

Kenyan Pawpaw Cake
Macadamia nuts and brown sugar top this cake, ideal with coffee

300 g (1½ cups) papaya, peeled, deseeded and sliced attractively
2 teaspoons lemon juice
1 tablespoon plain flour
1 tablespoon sugar
225 g (1¾ cups) self-raising flour
1 teaspoon baking powder
150 g (2/3 cup) sugar
2 large eggs, beaten
150 g (¾ cup) melted butter or margarine
½ teaspoon almond essence
30 g (2 tablespoons) macadamia nuts, roughly chopped
brown sugar

Mix papaya with lemon juice, flour and sugar. Set aside. Sift flour with baking powder and sugar. Combine the beaten eggs, melted margarine and almond essence. Mix wet ingredients with dry until smooth. Spread half the mixture over the base of a 22.5 cm (9 inch) cake tin. Arrange the prepared pawpaw over and dot with rest of cake mixture. Sprinkle with macadamia nuts and brown sugar. Bake (Gas Mark 3, 160°C, 325°F) for about 1½ hours until pale golden brown and shrinking away from the sides of the tin. Cool slightly before removing from tin. Serve warm with coffee or top with cream or ice cream.

Serves 8

The China Plate is a wonderful addition to up-market dining in Nairobi. With an elegant décor by designer Andrew MacNaughton, and an ambitious menu of Szechuan specialities, the restaurant has made an impact on the spoilt diners of Nairobi. Unlike most other Chinese restaurants, meat and vegetables are generally not mixed together. There are few thickeners in the sauces, and the dishes are beautifully, if simply garnished. All the preparation is last-minute, which means fresh food, served very hot. The Szechuan orientation means plenty of chillies, but you can vary the amounts according to taste.

Golden Fried Prawns   crispy queen prawns

Beef Green Pepper   stir-fried vegetables and beef

Toffee Bananas   caramelised deep-fried bananas

Golden Fried Prawns
Serve with sweet-and-sour sauce or chilli sauce

12 fresh queen size prawns
125 ml (½ cup) sherry
pinch of monosodium glutamate
   (optional)
1 teaspoon salt
100 g (¾ cup) flour
40 g (6 tablespoons) cornflour
1 teaspoon baking powder
salt and pepper
2 tablespoons oil
oil for deep frying

Shell the prawns leaving the tails intact. De-vein and wash well. Marinate in sherry, monosodium glutamate and salt and pepper for ½ hour. Make a smooth batter from the remaining ingredients, mixing well with water. Blend in the 2 tablespoons oil. Heat oil for deep frying. Dip prawns in batter. (To ensure that prawns are properly coated hold by tail.) Fry until golden brown and drain on absorbent kitchen towels. Serve immediately.

Serves 4

Beef Green Pepper
Use the leanest, tenderest beef possible

400 g (14 oz) beef fillet, thinly sliced
2 teaspoons cornflour
2 teaspoons soy sauce
pinch of salt
pinch of ground black pepper
pinch of monosodium glutamate
   (optional)

Marinate the sliced fillet in soy sauce, cornflour, salt, pepper, monosodium glutamate and half the beaten egg, for 30 minutes. Heat enough oil to deep fry the beef in a wok or deep frying pan. Deep fry the beef. Drain all but 1 teaspoon of the oil and toss the carrots and green peppers for 1-2 minutes. Remove with slotted spoon. Add chilli paste, soy sauce, salt, pepper and monosodium glutamate if desired. Add a little water to cook the sauce. Dissolve the cornflour in a little water and

1 egg, beaten
1 carrot, peeled and sliced diagonally
1 green pepper, sliced diagonally
1 teaspoon chilli paste (made from equal
 portions of chilli powder and fresh red
 chilli)
dash of soy sauce
pinch of salt, pepper and monosodium
 glutamate
cornflour to thicken

stir into sauce to thicken for ½ minute. Add the beef, carrots and green peppers. Serve at once accompanied by white rice.

Serves 3

Toffee Bananas

Serve with a pot of jasmin tea

4 ripe bananas
1 tablespoon cornflour
1 egg
2 tablespoons sifted flour
oil for deep frying
4 tablespoons sugar
1 tablespoon sesame seeds

Peel and cut the bananas in half lengthwise and then in half crosswise. Dust the pieces with cornflour shaking off any excess. Beat the egg, and add the sifted flour to make a smooth batter. Heat enough oil to deep fry the bananas in a wok or deep frying pan. Coat the banana pieces evenly in the prepared batter and deep fry until golden brown. Remove with a slotted spoon onto absorbent paper. Drain oil from wok and add water and sugar. Stir over medium heat to dissolve the sugar. Continue stirring until the sugar caramelises. Add fried banana and sprinkle sesame seeds. Coat well and remove. Dip the hot banana in iced water to harden the toffee and serve immediately.

Serves 4

El Patio

Spanish food is ideally suited to Kenya, where vegetables, seafood and wonderful fresh fruits are cheap and plentiful. No one does it better than the chefs at El Patio, a very Spanish restaurant in the modern Kenya Reinsurance Plaza. The décor is crisp and clean, and the atmosphere deliciously Mediterranean, particularly at night when the lighting is dim and the music romantic. Paella is a speciality of the house, along with chilled gazpacho and garlicky cazuela, a lovely seafood casserole. Masses of garlic bread and lightly dressed salads go well with Spanish food, along with carafes of chilled white wine or, better still, fruity Sangria.

Gazpacho   a chilled spicy vegetable soup

Paella   tender meat, chicken, seafood and golden rice

Cazuela de Mariscos   a moist, flavourful seafood dish

Gazpacho

Pass around the garnishes separately

1 kg (2 lb) ripe tomatoes, peeled and
   chopped
250 g (8 oz) cucumbers, finely chopped
200 g (7 oz) green peppers, finely chopped
500 ml (2 cups) tomato juice
1 tablespoon olive oil
1 tablespoon sherry
1 tablespoon sugar
salt to taste
1 clove garlic, crushed
black pepper
8-10 ice cubes

Keep aside ½ cup of tomatoes, cucumbers and green peppers for garnish. Put all ingredients in electric blender and blend at high speed for 30-40 seconds. Chill well. Serve in chilled bowls. Offer bowls of finely chopped cucumber, tomato, green peppper and garlic croutons for garnish.

Serves 6

Paella

Normally this dish is cooked in a special paella pan, but an ordinary frying pan will do

6 crab claws
6 large whole prawns
12 crayfish
200 g (8 oz) fillet steak, cubed
6 small chicken legs
100 g (4 oz) squid
100 g (4 oz) small shrimp
200 g (8 oz) onions, chopped

Bring a large pan of water to the boil. Add ½ tablespoon salt. Boil crab claws, prawns and crayfish until cooked. Keep aside for garnish. Heat half the oil in a large frying pan and cook beef cubes quickly, then remove. Add chicken legs and cook until done. Then fry shrimps and finally squid. Keep aside. Add remaining oil and sauté onions and leeks until transparent. Add chopped tomatoes and crushed garlic. Cook 5 minutes more. Remove from heat. Add green peppers and squid to pan and spread evenly. Arrange chicken legs on outside and heap shrimps in

50 g (2 oz) leeks, chopped
500 g (1¼ lb) tomatoes, peeled and chopped
3 cloves garlic, crushed
200 g (8 oz) green peppers
3 cups cooked yellow rice (coloured with pinch of saffron while cooking)
½ cup boiled peas
chopped parsley
½ cup oil

the centre of the pan. Spread rice over everything except shrimps. Spread peas over rice. Garnish with crab claws, large prawns and crayfish. Cover and place over very low heat until heated through (about 10 minutes). Sprinkle with parsley and serve immediately.

Serves 6

Cazuela de Mariscos

Perhaps even more delicious when reheated the next day!

6 crab claws
12 crayfish
½ cup oil
200 g (2 cups) onions, chopped
250 g (2 cups) tomatoes, peeled and chopped
3 cloves garlic, crushed
200 g (1 cup) mushrooms, sliced
250 g (8 oz) prawns, peeled
250 g (8 oz) squid
250 g (8 oz) fish fillets, cubed
250 g (8 oz) green peppers, chopped
250 ml (1 cup) white wine
salt and pepper to taste
parsley for garnish

Heat water in a large pan. Add ½ tablespoon salt. Boil crab claws and crayfish and put aside. Heat oil in a casserole dish and sauté onions until transparent. Add tomatoes and garlic and cook for 5 minutes. Add mushrooms, prawns and squid, cook for 3 minutes, then add fish, green peppers and wine. Add salt and pepper to taste. Simmer for 5 minutes. Add crab claws and crayfish and simmer, covered for a further 5 minutes. Sprinkle parsley on top and serve immediately with boiled white rice.

Serves 6

The Trattoria has long been a family favourite of ours. With its bustling atmosphere and vast menu of Italian goodies, it attracts everyone from tourists who wander in for an ice cream, to serious diners who start with soup and hot garlic toast and proceed right through the pasta and entrées to Mama Ruffo's lavish desserts. Mama Ruffo's son, Gaetano, is the man behind the Trattoria (and Visions Night Club). Recently, he has added the luxurious Foresta Magnetica in Nairobi's Corner House to his collection. It is decorated with stunning metallic trees, and the tables are laid with golden tablecloths, original glassware and place settings. The restaurant is an enchanting place for late-night dining to the delightful background music of the resident pianist. Gaetano has a completely different menu at each of his restaurants, and the recipes he and his Mama have shared reflect a homey Italian feeling.

Mama Ruffo's Asparagus Crepes   her "very best" recipe

Carpaccio   raw beef fillet marinated in lemon juice and olive oil

Spaghetti Ghiottona   pasta with anchovies, capers and mushrooms

Pollo alla Romana   a classic Italian chicken recipe

Hot Zabaglione   one of the most impressive desserts created

Banana Beau Harnais Flambé   caramelised whole bananas with rum

Mama Ruffo's Asparagus Crepes
Use tender young asparagus

50 g (1/3 cup) flour
30 g (2 tablespoons) melted butter
4 eggs
125 ml (½ cup) milk
pinch salt
25 g (1½ tablespoons) butter for frying
  crepes
500 g (1 lb) asparagus, trimmed
250 ml (1 cup) cream
125 g (½ cup) natural yoghurt
2 tablespoons grated Parmesan cheese
½ tablespoon butter
salt to taste

Wash and drain asparagus. Tie in bundles and cook in slightly salted water with spears pointing upwards. When points are tender, drain and cool. Cut green parts from stems. Prepare crepes in the following way: mix together flour with beaten eggs, melted butter and milk. Melt ½ tablespoon of remaining butter in a frying pan. Pour enough batter into pan to make a thin crepe and cook over medium heat until golden brown on one side. Turn and cook the other side. Put aside. To make the sauce, mix ¼ cup cream with the yoghurt. Spoon cream mixture onto each crepe, sprinkle with Parmesan cheese and top with asparagus points. Roll crepes so the filling is completely enclosed. Place in buttered dish. Cover with remaining cream and cheese and bits of butter. Place in moderate oven (Gas Mark 4, 180°C, 350°F), for 10 minutes. Serve in an open pan or dish with an asparagus tip on each crepe.

Serves 4

Carpaccio

Use the best quality fillet you can buy

225 g (8 oz) beef fillet, with the fat trimmed off
4 tablespoons lemon juice
1 tablespoon vinegar
4 tablespoons olive oil
freshly ground black pepper
4 tablespoons Parmesan cheese
fresh parsley, chopped

Wrap fillet in aluminium foil and half freeze. Slice as thinly as possible, across the grain. Arrange slices on two plates, overlapping to make an attractive presentation, pressing the slices down firmly. Keep chilled until serving time. To serve, cover the slices of beef completely with lemon juice, vinegar and olive oil. Grind black pepper on top and sprinkle with Parmesan cheese and parsley.

Serves 2

Spaghetti Ghiottona

A zesty Mediterranean pasta

4 tablespoons oil
4 anchovies
4 cloves garlic, chopped
1 green chilli, chopped
1 tablespoon capers
1 cup mushrooms, chopped
¼ cup olives, stoned and chopped (optional)
75 ml (¼ cup) dry white wine
1 medium tin (400 g) peeled tomatoes
400 g (1 lb) spaghetti

Heat oil in a frying pan and add anchovies, allowing them to "melt", releasing the oil. Add garlic and chillies and cook gently until soft. Add capers, mushrooms, and olives if desired. Meanwhile, put a large pot of salted water on to boil and cook pasta. Add wine to sauce, cover and simmer for 3-4 minutes. Add peeled tomatoes. Stir and cook another 5 minutes. When spaghetti is cooked al dente (just tender) drain and add to sauce. Toss spaghetti in sauce in a warmed serving bowl and top with freshly grated Parmesan and chopped fresh parsley.

Serves 4

Pollo alla Romana

Easy, colourful way to prepare chicken

1 chicken
3 tablespoons oil
1 onion, chopped
1 kg (2 lb) bell peppers (green, yellow and red), sliced into 6-8 rings each
1 leek, cut into 1.25 cm (½ inch) rounds
1 kg (2 lb) tomatoes, peeled and sliced
1 bay leaf
1 teaspoon salt

Cut chicken into portions. Heat oil in a frying pan. Fry chicken together with chopped onions and peppers. When lightly browned, add leeks, tomatoes, bay leaf and salt. Bake in moderate oven (Gas Mark 4, 180°C, 350°F) for 30 minutes or until chicken is tender. Serve with assorted seasonal vegetables and rice.

Serves 4

Hot Zabaglione

Serve in a champagne glass for maximum effect!

4 egg yolks
4 tablespoons castor sugar
60 ml (4 tablespoons) double cream
2 tots marsala wine or port
freshly grated nutmeg (optional)

Place all ingredients in a blender for 2 minutes to mix until fluffy. Pour into the top of a double boiler with boiling water beneath. Whisk constantly over moderate heat until thick and foamy. Pour into glasses immediately and serve. If desired, grate nutmeg on top.

Serves 2-3

Banana Beau Harnais Flambé
Flambé at the table!

4 ripe bananas
15 g (1 tablespoon) unsalted butter
90 g (6 tablespoons) sugar
125 ml (½ cup) double cream
45 ml (3 tablespoons) rum
freshly grated coconut for garnish

Melt butter in a frying pan. Add sugar and stir until the sugar caramelises and turns brown. Place peeled whole bananas in caramel sauce and when well coated, add cream. Cook gently until thickened. Add rum. Put a match to the mixture and flambé. Place in a serving dish and pour sauce over bananas. Sprinkle top with grated coconut.

Serves 2-4

Ibis Grill

Chef Eamon Mullan's recipes were first collected in the *Tastes of Kenya*. Since then, the inventive Irishman has created a whole new type of cuisine, combining the very finest of Kenyan ingredients with ideas from around the world, to create a unique Kenyan Nouvelle Cuisine. Together with Chef Thomas Kikozi, Eamon has turned the Ibis into a showcase for superb cooking and original presentation. The Ibis Grill is an ideal environment, with stunning wall hangings of ibises in flight and a view of the well-manicured Norfolk courtyard. Paintings by A.R. Thomson grace the walls of the bar area, and a new terrace makes it possible for diners to enjoy their meal in the open-air, a year-round treat in Nairobi.

Leek and Onion Flan with Basil Sauce   a most delicately flavoured quiche

Camembert Sauce for Vegetables   rich and lemony

Fillets Mignons with Roquefort Sauce   one of the Ibis's most popular dishes

Tea Parfait with Aniseed Sauce   chilled Pernod-flavoured desert

Leek and Onion Flan with Basil Sauce

A perfect light luncheon quiche

1 uncooked 20 cm (8 inch) pastry shell
30 g (2 tablespoons) butter
50 g (½ cup) leeks, cut into julienne strips
50 g (½ cup) white onion, finely sliced
2 eggs, beaten
125 ml (½ cup) cream
150 ml (½ cup) milk
pinch of nutmeg
dash of salt and white pepper
300 ml (1¼ cups) cream
50 ml (¼ cup) white wine
50 ml (¼ cup) chicken stock diluted with
    100 ml (1/3 cup) water
10 g (½ tablespoon) butter
several fresh basil leaves, finely shredded
salt and white pepper to taste

Melt butter in a large pan and sweat the leeks and onions until soft. Mix eggs, cream, milk and seasonings in a bowl. Place onions and leeks in the bottom of the pastry shell and cover with custard. Bake in a hot oven (Gas Mark 6, 200°C, 400°F) until firm to the touch. Prepare a sauce by reducing the cream and wine by one-third. Add chicken stock and reduce further, until the sauce has a velvety texture. Do not allow to boil again. At the last moment add butter and shredded basil. Season. Serve in a sauce boat alongside the flan.

Serves 6

Camembert Sauce

This sauce is delicious with deep-fried mushrooms or any cooked vegetable

180 g (6 oz) Camembert
125 ml (½ cup) Hollandaise sauce (see
    Guide to Ingredients)
200 ml (¾ cup) double cream, whipped
salt and pepper to taste

Place Camembert in a saucepan over water. Heat until the cheese has melted. Add to prepared Hollandaise sauce, whisking together until light. Fold whipped cream into the sauce and pour over vegetables. Place under grill until bubbly.

Makes 375 ml (1½ cups) sauce

Fillets Mignon with Roquefort Sauce
Use local blue cheese as a reasonable substitute for Roquefort

6 beef fillets, flattened
50 ml (3 tablespoons) oil
15 g (1 tablespoon) butter
50 ml (¼ cup) red wine
200 ml (¾ cup) demi-glacé sauce (*see
   below how to make alternative)
500 ml (2 cups) single cream
125 g (4 oz) Roquefort or less
salt and pepper to taste
chopped toasted nuts for garnish

Heat oil in a large frying pan. Add butter and fry the fillet as desired. Remove and keep warm. Pour off oil from the pan and add the red wine, followed by the demi-glacé. Stir in cream and cheese and reduce sauce until it coats the back of a spoon. Strain. Place fillets on a serving dish and pour sauce over. Top each fillet with chopped nuts. Serve with buttered pasta or rice.

*To make an alternative to demi-glacé sauce, fry the fillets and add two peeled, puréed tomatoes to the meat juices. Pour in a sherry glass of red wine and 1 beef stock cube. Cool 3-4 minutes until well blended and proceed with recipe.

Serves 6

Tea Parfait with Aniseed Sauce
A most sophisticated dessert

3 tea bags
200 ml (¾ cup) water
150 g (½ cup and 2 tablespoons) refined
   sugar
5 egg yolks
250 ml (1 cup) double cream
300 ml (1¼ cups) cream
30 g (2 tablespoons) sugar
2 tots (3 tablespoons) Pernod
green food colouring (optional)

Boil water, sugar and tea bags together until you have a tea syrup (approximately 7 minutes). In a separate bowl whisk the egg yolks and add the tea syrup very slowly. Allow to cool at room temperature. Whip the double cream. When the syrup has cooled completely, carefully fold the syrup into the cream. Pour into a mould and place in the freezer. To make the sauce whisk the cream, sugar, Pernod, and food colouring if desired. When mould has set, invert on a chilled platter and serve in slices topped with cream sauce and decorated with fresh mint leaves.

Serves 8

For a romantic evening at the coast, it is hard to beat a meal on the beautiful Imani Dhow, an intricately carved old sailing vessel which used to voyage between Zanzibar and Mombasa with a cargo of boriti poles, cotton and maize. Now beached on the grounds of the Severin Sea Lodge, she is manned by a crew of waiters garbed in traditional long white robes, called kanzus. The captain's quarters have been taken over by the bar and the guests dine in the open air on the refitted deck. Imani means "faith", no doubt required in large quantities to weather the Indian Ocean storms. To provide good luck, all Zanzibari dhows have the symbol of an eye painted on the side of the hull—and the Imani is no exception. It's obviously effective, for the food is delicious, reflecting the coast influences as far south as Zanzibar.

Pemba Soup   a rich seafood soup

Lobster Terrine   a light terrine combining lobster, prawns, chicken and meat

Coconut Parfait   a cool and dreamy ending

Pemba Soup

Serve with mahamri, traditional Swahili buns

200 g (¾ cup) butter
100 g (1 cup) chopped onions
200 g (7 oz) each of carrots, leeks and celery
   cut into julienne strips
200 g (7 oz) each of fresh lobster, prawns
    and kingfish, cleaned and diced
100 g brown beans, half cooked
50ml (3 tablespoons) white wine
pinch of Spanish saffron
pinch of turmeric
salt and pepper to taste
1 litre (4 cups) fish stock
2 fresh green chillies, chopped
100 ml (1/3 cup) fresh single cream
chopped fresh coriander (dhania)

In a large pot melt butter and sauté onions until soft. Add carrots, leeks and celery. Sauté for several minutes and then add shellfish, fish and beans. Add white wine and seasoning and simmer. Add fish stock. Cook slowly until all the vegetables and beans are tender. Finally add chillies and cream. Serve sprinkled with a few drops of Pernod and chopped fresh dhania.

Serves 6

Lobster Terrine

This is fussy to make, but makes a splendid cold starter which can be prepared well ahead

300 g (11 oz) kingfish fillets, cubed
300 g (11 oz) chicken legs, de-boned and
   cubed
40 g (1½ oz) lobster, cubed
50 g (2 oz) peeled king prawns
50 g (2 oz) mushrooms, finely chopped
125 ml (½ cup) fresh cream
75 ml (¼ cup) Noilly Prat liqueur
salt to taste
freshly ground black pepper
juice of 1 lemon (or to taste)
½ teaspoon Aromat Seasoning (Accent)
½ teaspoon Worcestershire sauce

Mix together Kingfish, chicken, lobster, prawns and mushrooms. Stir in cream and spices. Season with salt. Butter individual baking forms or one loaf pan. Fill with mixture. Place in a pan of water and bake for 45 minutes (or until a knife stuck into the centre of the mixture comes out clean) in a moderate oven (Gas Mark 4, 180°C, 350°F). Let cool. Chill in fridge and cut into slices. Garnish with lemon wedges.

Serves 6

Coconut Parfait

You need an electric beater or a strong arm and a whisk for this frozen dessert

3 eggs
5 egg yolks
100 g (½ cup) sugar
1 teaspoon vanilla
225 g (8 oz) grated coconut
500 ml (2 cups) fresh double cream

Beat egg yolks with whole eggs, sugar and vanilla in a bowl. Place in the top of a double boiler (Bain-Marie) and beat with an electric beater or whisk, over moderate heat until light and creamy. Remove from heat. Continue beating until cool. Whip cream until stiff. Fold in coconut. Fold egg yolk mixture with cream mixture and pour into a mould. Freeze until hard. Turn out on a platter and slice to serve.

Serves 6

Island Camp, Baringo

Escaping to Baringo Island ensures a rest for the soul and a treat for the palate. Set on Olkokwe Island in Lake Baringo, the camp offers a perfect escape for anyone tired of the rat race. The food is delicious—simple but well cooked—and the setting is sublime. The bar and dining area are set on the high point of the island overlooking the lake where hippos, crocodiles and an astonishing number of multi-coloured birds provide entertainment for the guests. Established in 1972, Island Camp remains a favourite get-away for locals who love the special atmosphere.

Chilled Avocado Soup   pale green and lemony

Chef Rotich's Pickled Fish   a tangy starter

Spinach Roulade   elegant yet surprisingly easy

Tilapia Beurre Noir   lake-fish with black butter and fresh herbs

Chilled Avocado Soup
Ideal for a summer's day

3 ripe avocados, peeled and stoned
juice of 1 lemon
750 ml (3 cups) chicken stock or bouillon
  cubes, cooled
salt and pepper to taste
dash of Worcestershire sauce
250 ml (1 cup) single cream
chopped chives for garnish

Place avocados and lemon juice in blender. Process until smooth, then gradually pour in cooled chicken stock. Season with salt and pepper to taste and add Worcestershire sauce. Transfer to a glass bowl and beat in cream. Chill until very cold. Serve in bowls, garnished with chopped chives and finely sliced avocado.

Serves 4-5

Chef Rotich's Pickled Fish
Served on camp barbecue nights as a starter

6 tilapia fillets
juice of 6 lemons
2 bay leaves
2 medium onions, sliced
pinch each of salt and pepper
4 cloves garlic, crushed

Slice the tilapia fillets into long, thin strips. Place in a bowl and cover with a mixture of lemon juice, chopped onions, crushed garlic, bay leaves and a pinch each of salt and pepper. Cover and leave in fridge for 4-5 hours. Drain and place fish in serving dish. Cover with sauce. (To make sauce, boil sugar and water together in a saucepan until brown and syrupy. Take off heat and stir in butter. When cool, stir in tomato sauce,

45 g (3 tablespoons) sugar
50 ml (3 tablespoons) water
15 g (1 tablespoon) butter
1 tablespoon tomato ketchup
3 tablespoons mayonnaise
3 tablespoons hard paw paw, chopped
2 tablespoons parsley

mayonnaise and chopped paw paw.) Sprinkle with chopped parsley and serve as a starter with brown bread.

Serves 6

Spinach Roulade
Ideal as an appetizer or cold buffet dish

300 g (2 cups) cooked, drained and finely
    chopped spinach
30 g (2 tablespoons) butter
salt and pepper to taste
½ teaspoon nutmeg, grated
60 g (½ cup) grated Parmesan cheese
5 eggs
240 g (1 cup) cream cheese
150 g (¾ cup) smoked sailfish paté
    (optional)
1 tablespoon chopped chives

Pre-heat oven (Gas Mark 4, 180°C, 350°F). Line a 30 cm (12 inch) Swiss roll tin with grease-proof paper. Heat spinach in a pan with the butter, salt, pepper, nutmeg and 2/3 of the cheese. Separate eggs and beat yolk and white separately. Whites should be stiff, but not dry. Beat spinach into yolks. Fold in whites. Pour into tin and bake for approximately 20 minutes, or until the top is firm. Cool for about 2 hours. Turn out and remove paper. Spread with cream cheese, smoked sailfish paté and chives in alternate strips across the short side of the base. Sprinkle with remaining Parmesan cheese. Roll starting along the long side of the roll. Chill and cut into slices.

Serves 6

Tilapia Beurre Noir
A delicate way to serve lake-fish

1¼ litres (5 cups) chicken stock
4 sticks celery, chopped
4 carrots, chopped
2 tablespoons vinegar
1 teaspoon salt
tilapia fillets for six
90 g (1/3 cup) butter
3 tablespoons chopped, fresh dill
3 tablespoons chopped, fresh parsley
juice of ½ lemon

Pour chicken stock into a saucepan and add chopped celery and carrots. Boil 10-15 minutes. Add vinegar and salt. Place fillets in the stock and boil gently for 5-10 minutes, until just cooked through. Remove and drain off stock. Place in oven-proof serving dish. Heat butter in a saucepan until dark brown. Pour over the fish. Top with chopped fresh herbs. Squeeze lemon juice over the fillets and serve immediately.

Serves 6

Jax

Located in the heart of Nairobi's city centre, Jax is famous for clean, healthy and original food. Goan curries share the hot table with splendid continental-style quiches, English pies, Portuguese fish and even sumptuous dishes with an oriental flair. The salads are equally varied and interesting, as are the home-made breads, cakes and puddings. Phyllis and Peter Costabir oversee the food and the customers with an eagle eye. Their speciality, Goan cuisine, represents a delectable blend of Portuguese and Indian influences from the tiny state of Goa, on the west coast of India.

Mole   ginger and garlic flavoured pickled fish

Shakuthi   intriguing Goan chicken curry

Goan Pullau   moist rice fragrant with cinnamon, cloves, almonds and turmeric

Alebele   pancakes stuffed with coconut sauce

Mole

Serve this traditional Goan pickled fish as a starter with hot bread

1 kg (2 lb) firm mackerel or similar fish
1 2.5-cm (2-inch) piece ginger, crushed
1 clove garlic, crushed
1 tablespoon paprika
1 tablespoon chilli powder
1 tablespoon curry powder
1 teaspoon salt
½ cup vegetable oil
500 ml (2 cups) malt vinegar

Cut mackerel into small portions and fry until crisp. Mix together all remaining ingredients except for oil and vinegar. Heat ½ cup oil in a large pan and pour in the paste. Simmer to blend. Add vinegar and cook for approximately 5 minutes. Add fish. Remove from fire and place in a large sterilized jar. Leave to mature approximately 4 weeks.

Serves 10

Shakuthi

Great chicken curry, serve with rice or chapatis

1 medium chicken, cut into portions
2 tablespoons oil
2 medium onions, sliced
2 teaspoons cumin
2 teaspoons coriander seed
10 black peppercorns
3 tablespoons desiccated coconut
2 tablespoons tomato puree

Place chicken, oil and onion in a large pan and simmer, covered, for 10 minutes. Place cumin seed, coriander seed, coconut and peppercorns under a grill and cook until browned. Cool and grind in a coffee grinder. Add tomato puree, ginger, garlic, coconut slices, paprika, turmeric, sliced green chilli and broiled spices, to chicken. Continue cooking gently to blend. Add vinegar, salt, sugar and water. Cook (covered) until meat is tender.

12.5-cm (1-inch) piece ginger, crushed
4 cloves garlic, crushed
a few slices of coconut (broiled or grilled)
1 tablespoon paprika powder
½ tablespoon turmeric powder
1 green chilli, sliced
2 tablespoons vinegar
½ teaspoon salt
1 teaspoon sugar
375 ml (1½ cups) water

Serves 4

Goan Pullau

Garnish this delightful rice dish with sliced bananas before serving

450 g (2 cups) Basmati rice
1 large onion, sliced
3 tablespoons vegetable oil
4 5-cm (2-inch) sticks cinnamon bark
10 whole black peppercorns
6 whole cloves
½ teaspoon turmeric powder
pinch of saffron
120 g (¾ cup) raisins
60 g (¼ cup) almonds
1 litre (4 cups) water
salt to taste
bananas for garnish

Wash rice, drain and put aside. Fry onions in oil in a large pan. Add whole spices and when well blended, turn down heat. Add remaining ingredients, including washed rice and boil rapidly for 10 minutes. Cover and finish cooking in a hot oven until grains are tender.

Serves 8

Alebele
Traditional Goan crepe with coconut filling

120 g (2 cups) desiccated coconut
1 tablespoon castor sugar
2 tablespoons black treacle
60 ml (4 tablespoons) water
180 g (1½ cups) flour
2 eggs
dash of salt
250 ml (1 cup) milk
250 ml (1 cup) water
oil for frying
lemon wedges for garnish

Place first four ingredients in a saucepan and bring to a boil. Turn down and simmer until thickened slightly. Stir together flour, eggs, salt and combined milk and water until light and foamy. Lightly oil a non-stick frying pan and heat until a drop of batter sizzles. Pour batter in to cover base of pan. Fry gently until cooked. Slide on to a plate and fill with coconut sauce. Roll up and arrange on a heated plate. Garnish with lemon wedges and serve hot.

Serves 4

Khyber

First time visitors to the Khyber are enchanted by the quality of the decor, the graciousness of the service and the elegance of the Mughlai cuisine. Devised for the conquering Mughal Emperors, the dishes are exquisite and labour intensive, generally prepared with expensive ingredients, like butter, cream, almonds and imported spices. The Khyber's food tends to be lighter than that found at other Mughal restaurants in town, a welcome change for most of us. The dishes take time to prepare, but it's worth the effort for the results are delicious and should establish your reputation as an adventurous and talented cook!

Rashmi Kebab   tender minced chicken kebabs

Kofta aloo Bukhara   potato and cottage cheese dumplings in a rich sauce

Machli Haryali   especially for dieters, fillet of fish baked in green masala

Murgh Sultan   chicken fit for a sultan

Reshmi Kebab
The Khyber's version of a popular Indian starter

1 kg (2 lb) boneless chicken
25 g (1 tablespoon) crushed garlic
25 g (1 tablespoon) freshly grated ginger
6 tablespoons chopped coriander (dhania)
   leaves
3 tablespoons chopped fresh mint leaves
2 medium onions, chopped
4 green chillies (or to taste)
½ tablespoon salt
½ tablespoon turmeric
1 tablespoon chilli powder
2 teaspoons melted butter

Make a paste of garlic, ginger, coriander and mint. Mix together all remaining ingredients including chicken and put into blender. Blend all, adding garlic paste, until finely minced. Press ¼ cup of the mixture at a time on to skewers and barbecue on a charcoal grill or under a gas or electric grill until browned. Place skewers on a heated plate. brush with melted butter and serve.

Serves 6

Kofta aloo Bukhara
A royal treat

500 g (1 lb) potatoes, peeled
500 g (1 lb) cottage cheese (panir)
25 g (1 tablespoon) freshly grated ginger
2 tablespoons chopped green chillies
2 tablespoons gram flour
oil for frying

Boil the potatoes until tender. Remove skins and mash with cottage cheese, 1 teaspoon grated ginger, 1 teaspoon chopped chillies, gram flour and a little salt to taste. Mash mixture by hand thoroughly and make into small balls, or koftas. Heat oil in a large saucepan until right for deep frying. Fry koftas until golden brown. Put aside. Melt butter in a saucepan. Place chopped onions in a blender and blend till a paste. Add

250 g (1 cup) butter
150 g (1½ cups) chopped onions
40 g (2 tablespoons) crushed garlic
200 g (7 oz) tomatoes, puréed
1 tablespoon red chilli powder
1 tablespoon coriander powder
½ tablespoon turmeric
60 g (¼ cup) cashew nuts
300 ml (1¼ cups) milk
100 ml (1/3 cup) cream

garlic, ginger, tomato purée, turmeric, chilli powder and coriander. Mix well and add to the butter. Cook for 5 minutes. While cooking, blend cashew nuts to a paste. Add to cooked spice and butter mixture, together with milk and salt. Cook another 10 minutes or longer, until flavours are well blended. Remove from fire and add cream. Finally, add koftas. Heat through, taking care not to boil. Serve with a garnish of cream on top.

Serves 6

Machli Haryali

Coconut and coriander give a fresh liveliness to this excellent, light fish recipe

1 kg (2 lb) fish fillets
250 g (8 oz) fresh coriander leaves (dhania)
125 g (4 oz) fresh mint leaves
6 green chillies (or less)
2 tablespoons jeera (cumin)
5 tablespoons grated coconut
1 tablespoon salt
1 tablespoon crushed garlic
2 tablespoons freshly chopped ginger
2 tablespoons oil
juice of 6 limes

Cut fish into four fillets and place in a bowl. Make a masala by placing coriander, mint and chillies in a blender. Add jeera, coconut, salt, garlic and ginger. Blend to fine paste. Add 1 tablespoon oil and lime juice to masala. Coat fish with spice mixture and leave to marinate for 30 minutes. Coat the bottom of a large cooking pan with oil. Heat the pan in the oven till very hot. Put the fish in the hot oil for 2 minutes. Then bake in moderate oven (Gas Mark 4, 180°C, 350°F) for 15 minutes or until fish is cooked but not dry.

Serves 4

Murgh Sultan

A unique chicken recipe from the Khyber's chef

1 kg (2 lb) chicken, de-boned
250 g (1 cup) butter
150 g (1½ cups) chopped onion
75 g (3 tablespoons) crushed garlic
50 g (2 tablespoons) freshly grated ginger
1 tablespoon red chilli powder
½ tablespoon turmeric powder
1 tablespoon ground coriander powder
250 g (8 oz) tomatoes
2 green peppers, chopped
1 tablespoon cumin
salt to taste
4 tablespoons chopped coriander leaves (dhania)
1 teaspoon garam masala (see Guide to Ingredients)
juice of 2 limes

Melt butter in a cooking pot. Add chopped onions and fry till golden. Add garlic and ginger and cook till softened. Add chilli, turmeric, coriander powder and saute for a few minutes. Add chopped tomatoes, green pepper, cumin and a little salt. Cook for 3 minutes. Add chicken and cover. Cook over low fire for 5-10 minutes. Remove lid and add chopped coriander leaves, garam masala and lime juice. Cook, half covered until chicken is done, adding more water if necessary. Garnish with thin slivers of ginger and chopped coriander leaves.

Serves 4

La Galleria always comes as a surprise to first time visitors. Located on the ground floor of the International Casino in Nairobi, the restaurant's décor has a vaguely oriental feel to it, though the cooking is strictly Italian and the superb view is of tropical trees and flowering bushes. Chef Renzo presides over the restaurant and its sister the Toona Tree. This is an open air marvel with a 40-foot high makuti roof, beautiful hand-crafted wooden tables with charcoal grills carved out of the centres, low-slung leather chairs and a children's playground featuring glorious Makonde sculptures. The food at both restaurants is honest, hearty and delicious ... and easy to prepare at home.

Riso Pilau   superb shrimp sauce over fluffy rice

Renzo's Tomato Sauce   an essential sauce

Sardinian Prawns   prawns gratinéed in Bechamel sauce

Spaghetti Scoglio   a delightful seafood spaghetti

Crepes Grand Marnier   rich, buttery crepes

Riso Pilau
Delicately seasoned, a perfect luncheon dish

30 g (2 tablespoons) butter
2 tablespoons chopped onions
1 clove garlic, finely chopped
60 g (2 oz) shrimps, cleaned and peeled
1 tablespoon cognac
2 tablespoons white wine
2 tablespoons Renzo's tomato sauce (recipe
   follows)
1 small red pepper, finely chopped
1 tablespoon fresh peas
60 ml (¼ cup) fresh cream
salt and pepper to taste
2 cups cooked rice
parsley for garnish

Heat the butter in a frying pan. Fry onion until golden. Add garlic and fry till soft and golden. Stir in shrimps. Pour in cognac and flambé by lighting a match and holding it near the liquid in the pan. Stir in white wine over moderate heat. When evaporated add the chopped peppers, peas and tomato sauce and cook for 5 minutes. Then add the cream. Gently cook another 3 minutes or until shrimps are cooked. Remove and serve on top of a bed of rice. Garnish with parsley.

Serves 2

Renzo's Tomato Sauce
Keep some in the fridge for emergencies

1 medium onion, chopped
1 tablespoon olive oil
500g (1 lb) tomatoes, peeled and chopped
1 bay leaf
½ teaspoon sugar
salt and pepper to taste

Heat oil in frying pan. Sauté onions until softened. Add tomatoes, bay leaf, sugar, salt and pepper. Simmer for 15-20 minutes.

Makes 2 cups

Sardinian Prawns
Serve golden brown and bubbly

6 jumbo or queen-sized prawns, boiled and
    shelled
30 g (2 tablespoons) butter
1 clove garlic, chopped
30 g (1 oz) mushrooms, chopped
1 tablespoon white wine
dash of Worcestershire sauce
2 tablespoons tomato sauce
2 tablespoons Bechamel or white sauce
juice of 1 lemon
salt and pepper to taste
60 g (¾ cup) finely grated breadcrumbs
1 tablespoon chopped parsley

Heat the butter until foamy in a small frying pan. Fry mushrooms and garlic for 2 minutes. Add white wine and cook until evaporated. Add Worcestershire sauce, tomato sauce, Bechamel sauce and lemon juice. Cook another 2 minutes until sauce is creamy. Season with salt and pepper to taste. Place prawns in an ovenproof dish. Spoon sauce over prawns. Mix breadcrumbs and parsley and place over prawns. Put in hot oven (Gas Mark 6, 200°C, 400°F) until crumbs are golden brown and sauce is bubbly.

Serves 2

Spaghetti Scoglio
Vary the seafood according to what's available or affordable

300 g (¾ lb) spaghetti
1 tablespoon oil (olive oil is preferred)
¼ cup shrimps, peeled and de-veined
¼ cup oysters
¼ cup lobster chunks

Clean seafood and set aside. Bring a large pan of salted water to the boil. Toss in spaghetti. It should cook in around 9-10 minutes, long enough to prepare the seafood sauce. Heat oil in a large frying pan. Fry garlic and chilli until soft. Add seafood and cook 2 minutes, turning gently. Add white wine. When evaporated, add tomato sauce and bay leaf. Simmer

½ cup seafish in cubes
2 cloves garlic, chopped
½ chilli pepper, chopped
1 tablespoon white wine
1 cup tomato sauce
1 bay leaf
salt and pepper to taste
1 tablespoon chopped parsley

for 5 minutes, or until seafood is completely cooked, but not soft. Add chopped parsley and serve over spaghetti, cooked al dente, or till firm.

Serves 2

Crepes Grand Marnier
Unbelievably sinful!

2 eggs
30 g (¼ cup) flour
grated peel of 1 orange
15 g (1 tablespoon) sugar
30 g (2 tablespoons) butter
4 egg yolks
60 g (½ cup) flour
150 g (1 cup and 2 tablespoons) sugar
½ teaspoon vanilla essence
500 ml (2 cups) milk
grated peel of 1 orange
1 teaspoon butter
1 tot Grand Marnier
1 tot brandy

In a bowl, mix together eggs and flour and beat until thick. Stir in finely grated orange peel and sugar. Heat butter till foamy in a frying pan. Pour in batter to make a thin crepe. Cook until bubbly and turn over, cook on other side. Repeat to make eight crepes. To prepare the sauce, mix together egg yolks, flour, sugar and vanilla in a bowl. Put aside. Pour milk into a saucepan with grated orange peel. Bring to a boil. Pour boiling liquid into egg mixture. Mix well and return to the pan. Boil for 1-2 minutes, stirring constantly. Remove from heat and cool. When cold, arrange the crepes in an ovenproof dish. Fill with sauce and fold over. Top with bits of butter and heat until very hot. Pour over Grand Marnier and brandy and touch a match to the surface to flambé the crepes. Serve immediately.

Serves 4

Le Chevalier

Rolf Schmid is one of those tireless inventors who is never happy unless he is contemplating a new project. Currently, he is running the cozy Horseman Restaurant in Karen and has become the country's leader in film catering, as well as presiding over Nairobi's most chic new restaurant, Le Chevalier. Designed to give Muthaiga's diplomatic community the incentive to dine out, Le Chevalier is luxuriously decorated with gorgeous upholstery, highly polished furniture, masses of silver and discreet hunting prints. Rolf may look a shade out of place in the environment, with his broad shoulders and a huge personality which dominates everything. His food is original and fun, always presented with great flair and attention to colour, texture and form.

Potato, Leek and Herb Soup   complex flavours in a hearty soup

Quails a la Kuki   quail in olive oil and herbs

Potato, Leek and Herb Soup
Use fresh herbs for the best results

500 g (1 lb) beef bones
bones of 1 chicken
2 litres (8 cups) water
300 g (10 oz) leeks, cleaned
200 g (7 oz) potatoes, cut into pieces
1 stalk celery
4 beef cubes
1 small bunch parsley
1 small bunch dill
1 bunch spinach
2 basil leaves
1 branch marjoram
1 branch thyme
2 tablespoons tarragon
½ cup chopped celery leaves
60 ml (¼ cup) yoghurt
250 ml (1 cup) cream

Boil bones, water, leeks, potatoes, celery and beef cubes together for about 90 minutes. When cool, process potatoes, leeks and celery in a processor or in a blender until totally puréed. Set aside. Next process the herbs and remaining ingredients except the cream. Place the potato purée in a pot and heat soup up to boiling point and add herb purée and cream. Correct seasonings.

Serves 8

Quails a la Kuki

Rolf credits Kuki Galman with this recipe

5 quails
500 ml (2 cups) white wine vinegar
6 cloves garlic
2 bay leaves
1 small bunch basil
1 twig fresh thyme
1 twig fresh marjoram
1 teaspoon crushed peppercorn
250 ml (1 cup) olive oil
10 green olives
10 black olives
½ teaspoon salt

Bring vinegar to a boil in a large saucepan. Add first six ingredients. Boil until quail is soft (approximately 30 minutes). Leave to cool. Drain liquid, and save for salad dressing. De-bone quail and place in a gratin dish. Garnish with olives. Add olive oil until quail is covered. Refrigerate until needed.

Serves 5

Since 1964 Mr Jehangir Cooper has been in the restaurant business. First he founded the Oriental Restaurant—then the Maharaja, a landmark on Kimathi Street, before he moved to his current premises down the road from the City Market in Nairobi. Mr Cooper knows how to make people comfortable by creating a welcoming, relaxed environment, and offering reasonably priced, well-cooked food served by cheerful waiters. His clientele is faithful, and includes some of the country's most respected legal minds. The food is still closely supervised, and in many cases, is cooked by Mr Cooper himself, using masalas he blends daily.

Fish Bhajia Maharaja   light, spicy fried fish

Green Masala Fried Prawns   truly a speciality of the house

Kashmiri Kulfi   saffron-tinged ice cream

Fish Bhajia Maharaja

Serve as an hors d'oeuvre with a choice of chutneys

10-12 tablespoons gram flour
2 teaspoons crushed garlic
¼ teaspoon salt
¼ teaspoon crushed green chillies
¼ teaspoon masala powder (see Guide to Ingredients)
500 g (1 lb) fresh Nile perch fillets
oil for deep frying

Mix flour with seasoning and water to make a batter. Cut fish fillets into bite-size pieces. Heat enough oil in a pan to deep fry. Dip the fish pieces in batter and deep fry. Remove with slotted spoon to a paper towel to absorb excess oil and keep hot in a warm oven. Serve immediately with limes and chutney.

Serves 6

Green Masala Fried Prawns

Vary the chillies according to taste

750 g (1¼ lb) fresh medium sized prawns (white Black Tiger prawns are best)
4-5 tablespoons oil
2 small red onions, finely chopped
2 teaspoons crushed garlic
¼ teaspoon salt
1 teaspoon tomato purée
1 teaspoon masala (see Guide to Ingredients) crushed together with 1 green chilli

Clean, shell and de-vein prawns. Heat oil in a large saucepan. Brown onions over moderate heat until golden. Add garlic, salt, tomato paste and mixture of Kashmiri masala and green chilli. Coat prawns with mixture and cook prawns over low fire until browned and cooked, about 7 minutes. Serve on a warmed serving dish with tandoori nan or chapatis, not with rice.

Serves 6

Kashmiri Kulfi

Cardamom and saffron give this refreshing dessert its exotic flavour

12 cups fresh whole milk
pinch of Kashmiri or Spanish saffron
¼ teaspoon ground fresh nutmeg
¼ teaspoon ground fresh cardamom
½ cup white sugar
2 teaspoons almonds, skinned and chopped
125 g (1 cup) cashew nuts, finely chopped

Boil milk over a low fire, stirring occasionally to prevent boiling over. Add saffron on first boil. Reduce to half the quantity, cooking for approximately 1 hour. Add seasonings and sugar, correcting sweetness if necessary. Add nuts and remove from heat. When completely cooled pour into kulfi moulds or conical freezer containers and freeze. When ready to serve remove from moulds by rolling in the palm of hand and tapping smartly out onto plate. Serve sliced.

Serves 6

Makaa Grill

I make no secret of the fact that I love the Makaa Grill, and greatly admire its inventive Scottish chef, Gordon Gorman. His recipes are magical, making creative use of local ingredients in a style he has named "New Kenyan Classical Cuisine". Gordon Gorman has taken on the job of Group Executive Chef for the Alliance Hotel Group, which has added the splendid Safari Beach Hotel to its string of hotels across the country. A host of dignitaries and personalities have dined at the Makaa and its new sister grill room at the Safari Beach Hotel. Most, says Gordon, are presented with a copy of my first *Specialities of the House,* in which his recipes are enthusiastically featured.

Tanga Crab and Melon Cocktail　a spicy seafood starter

Naro Moro Trout Mousse　an extravagantly creamy mousse

Noodles with Smoked Sailfish　superb seafood pasta

Chicken Africana　spinach and bacon-stuffed chicken breasts

Fillet of Pork with Malindi Pineapple　pork seasoned with curry, cream and Calvados

Swahili Fruit Pilau　coastal rice with fruit and nuts

Chocolate and Mango Terrine Mount Kenya　absolutely unique

Tanga Crab and Melon Cocktail

Fresh, light and original

2 medium sized ripe honeydew, cantaloupe,
    Garissa or flamingo melons
2 kg (4 lb) boiled crab
2 ripe avocados, halved
2 limes
1 teaspoon chilli sauce
1 tablespoon natural yoghurt
salt and pepper to taste

Cut the melons into equal halves and remove the seeds. Fill each half with cooked crab meat and chill in refrigerator until ready to serve. Make the sauce by placing the flesh of the avocado, juice of the limes, chilli sauce, and yoghurt in a blender. Mix well and season. If the sauce is blended too long it may become too thin. This can be remedied by folding a small amount of unsweetened whipped double cream into the mixture. To serve, remove the crab filled melon halves from the refrigerator and set in bowls of crushed ice garnished with a variety of exotic flowers or colourful leaves. Pour the sauce over the crab meat and garnish with crab legs or a few prawns.

Serves 4

Naro Moro Trout Mousse

Expensive but worth the investment

4 trout (or substitute Nile perch or tilapia)
2 egg whites
½ teaspoon salt
pinch of paprika
pinch of nutmeg
pinch of freshly chopped dill

Fillet the trout removing skin and bones. Combine the flesh with the egg white, salt, paprika, nutmeg, chopped dill, pepper and lime juice. Blend together in a blender or in a mortar. Pass the mixture through a fine sieve and set aside. Beat the cream until light and fluffy. Place the purée in a bowl and stand the bowl in a larger bowl filled with ice. With a rubber spatula gently fold in beaten cream, tablespoon by tablespoon, until the

ground black pepper to taste
2 limes
250 ml (1 cup) double cream, beaten
6 puff pastry medallions
12 cooked fresh water crayfish (optional)
sprigs of fresh dill to garnish

mixture is light and fluffy. Pour into individual or a single buttered mould and cover and set in a roasting pan. Pour enough boiling water into the tray to reach halfway up the side of the moulds, and bake in a moderate oven (Gas Mark 4, 180°C, 350°F) for approximately 20 minutes. To serve, unmould onto the pastry medallions, garnish with crayfish, sprigs of dill and caviar if you are feeling extravagant. Serve with sauce Hollandaise, sauce Americaine, or a fresh dill cream sauce.

Serves 6

Noodles with Smoked Sailfish Sauce

Substitute smoked salmon if necessary

100 g (5 tablespoons) unsalted butter
1 clove garlic, crushed
1 small onion, finely chopped
1 pinch freshly grated ginger
100 g (4 oz) chopped smoked sailfish
400 g (1 lb) tinned or fresh tomatoes,
  peeled and chopped
60 ml (¼ cup) dry white wine
125 ml (½ cup) double cream or natural
  yoghurt
salt and ground black pepper to taste
2 tablespoons Parmesan cheese
400 g (1 lb) green and white noodles,
  spaghetti or tagliatelle
1 teaspoon freshly chopped parsley

Melt the butter in a thick bottomed non-stick saucepan or frying pan. Add the garlic, onion and ginger and sauté until soft, taking care not to brown the onions. Cut the smoked sailfish into matchstick-size strips and add to the garlic and onions and stir gently for 2-3 minutes. Add the drained, chopped tomatoes, white wine and ½ cup of the tomato juice and allow to simmer gently until the sauce is reduced by one third. Do not stir with a sharp spoon. Simply shake the pan to prevent sticking. Constant stirring will break up the sailfish. Add the cream (or yoghurt), one spoonful of the Parmesan, chopped parsley, salt and pepper to taste. Simmer gently for a further 2-3 minutes. Cook the pasta in plenty of rapidly boiling salted water until just tender (al dente) and drain. Arrange the pasta on a serving plate and pour over the sauce. Sprinkle the remaining Parmesan and chopped parsley over the sauce.

Serves 4

Chicken Africana
One of the Makaa Grill's best selling dishes

4 supremes of chicken breast
180 g (6 oz) spinach
2 bananas
4 cloves garlic, crushed
4 grilled rashers lean bacon
100 g (1/3 cup) butter, melted
pinch of fresh grated ginger
2 beaten eggs
250 ml (1 cup) milk seasoned with salt and
    pepper
60 g (½ cup) seasoned flour
60 g (½ cup) cashew nuts, ground
30 g (¼ cup) breadcrumbs

Cut a small pouch in each of the chicken breasts deep enough to insert the filling. Finely chop spinach, bananas and bacon and combine with butter, garlic and ginger. Insert as much of this mixture as possible in each pocket and seal with the beaten out fillet attached to the supreme. Refrigerate until firm (1-2 hours). Carefully dust each supreme with seasoned flour and dip into a mixture of beaten eggs and seasoned milk. Combine breadcrumbs and cashews on a plate. Dip supremes into mixture and refrigerate another 10-20 minutes or until firm. Deep fry in medium hot oil. Serve with a fresh garlic and tomato sauce, a chilled yogurt and cucumber sauce or a sauce Hollandaise.

Serves 4

Fillet of Pork with Malindi Pineapple
If Calvados is unavailable substitute local brandy

75 g (1/3 cup) butter
500 g (1 lb) trimmed pork or veal fillet cut
    into escalopes
125 ml (½ cup) cider
3 tablespoons apple brandy (Calvados)

Heat butter in a shallow non-stick pan over low heat. Season escalopes with salt and pepper. Gently cook for 1 minute on each side and remove from pan. Pour off excess butter and add cider. Reduce by half and add brandy, escalopes, curry sauce, mango chutney and pineapple. Simmer gently for 2-3 minutes. Add cream, stirring in gently. Do not boil or

125 ml (½ cup) mild curry sauce
125 ml (½ cup) double cream
1 tablespoon mango chutney
250 g (8 oz) pineapple, cut into matchstick
    strips
100 g (½ cup) toasted flaked almonds
salt and pepper to taste

sauce may separate. Place contents of pan into a shallow ovenproof serving dish and sprinkle over toasted almonds and chopped parsley. Brown under a salamander.

Serves 4

Swahili Fruit Pilau

A Scot's interpretation of coastal rice

50 g (2½ tablespoons) unsalted butter
½ sweet green pepper, diced
½ sweet red pepper, diced
½ teaspoon freshly grated ginger
1 tablespoon roasted and chopped cashew
    nuts
pinch of chopped coriander (dhania) leaves
1 tablespoon mango chutney
2 tablespoons freshly grated coconut
1 tablespoon sultanas
1 firm, slightly under-ripe mango
½ mountain paw paw, diced
2 slices pineapple, diced
2 tablespoons fresh coconut milk
2 tablespoons papaya wine (optional)
4 cups cooked rice
salt and pepper to taste

Using a thick bottomed saucepan, or a medium sized non-stick frying pan, melt the butter over gentle heat. Add the peppers, ginger, cashews and coriander. Fry gently for 2-3 minutes, stirring frequently. Add mango chutney, grated coconut, sultanas, mango, pineapple, paw paw, coconut milk and papaya wine. Stir gently for 2 minutes. Add the cooked rice ensuring that the grains have separated. If your confidence permits, gently toss the contents of the pan until the rice and ingredients are thoroughly mixed. (Do not be tempted to use a wooden spoon or spatula. This will only result in squashing the rice and fruits into an unrecognisable and unappetising mess.) When thoroughly mixed, pop into a buttered tray or an oven-proof dish and finish in a medium oven by cooking for 5-10 minutes. To serve, add a few slices of untrimmed pineapple around the dish with a sprinkling of chopped dhania or parsley.

Serves 4

Chocolate and Mango Terrine Mount Kenya
Substitute any coffee liqueur for Kenya Gold

180 g (6 oz) Bourneville or cooking
   chocolate
4 tablespoons milk
zest of orange
1½ tablespoons Kenya Gold
6 egg yolks
90 g (1/3 cup) castor sugar
125 g (½ cup) sugar
250 ml (1 cup) water
1 tablespoon gelatine
310 ml (1¼ cups) double cream
3 large mangoes, sliced

Break chocolate into small pieces. Place in stainless steel pan with milk and grated orange zest. Melt over boiling water. Add liqueur. In a separate pan, whisk together egg yolks and sugar. When the chocolate has completely melted, add to the egg and sugar mixture and whisk over very low heat until it starts to thicken. Make sugar syrup by boiling together sugar and water until thickened, about 5 minutes. Melt ½ the gelatine in 1 tablespoon sugar syrup and add to mixture. Whisk cream until stiff, then fold very gently into the chocolate mixture and chill. Select a few nice pieces of mango and put aside for garnish. Boil remaining mangoes in the remaining sugar syrup until soft. Add softened remaining gelatine and blend in liquidiser. When chocolate mixture is almost set, pour half into small loaf tin and cool to set. When set, pour in mango jelly and sliced mangoes and cool to set. Pour on remainder of chocolate mixture and cool. When set, the terrine may be turned out by immersing for a few seconds in warm water. Slice with a warm knife and arrange on a plate with a little chocolate sauce and mango purée.

Serves 4

Mara Intrepids

Intrepids offers an experience of incomparable luxury in the wilds. The camp, one of the newest in the Mara, is a study in rustic elegance, with stunning tents filled with hand-crafted furniture, four-poster beds Karen Blixen would have died for, military trunks and grand closets for your crumpled khakis. Lunches are served outside in the shade, while dinners are served in a semi-enclosed, rock-floored dining area. The buffet lunches are large and imaginative, presented with style and originality. The pastries are unusually delicious, prepared by a young Kenyan chef who has spent many years studying French techniques. The experience cannot fail to be one which will provide cocktail party conversation for many years to come.

Fillet of Nile Perch with Sweet Red Peppers and Fennel   a colourful fish course

Roast Leg of Lamb Marinade   fresh herbs are best for this savoury roast

Pear and Ginger Tart   ideal for tart Kenya pears

Fillet of Nile Perch with Sweet Red Peppers and Fennel
Delicate presentation is essential

8 escalopes of Nile perch, well trimmed
8 large firm fresh red peppers
30 g (2 tablespoons) butter
25 g (¼ cup) chopped onions
1 large fennel, trimmed
fish stock (prepared by boiling trimmings
   with seasoning)
salt, pepper and cayenne pepper to taste
¼ teaspoon thyme
250 ml (1 cup) single cream
2 large whole red pimentos
1 small bunch chives, chopped

Roast red peppers in a hot oven (Gas Mark 6, 200°C, 400°F) until skins appear nearly burnt. Cool, remove skins, cut in half and remove seeds. Melt butter in a pan and sauté onions and half the quantity of fennel (chopped) until tender, but not coloured. Add enough fish stock to cover, and season with salt, pepper, cayenne and thyme. Half cover and simmer for ½ hour. Cool slightly and place in a blender. Strain. Add cream and return to pan over low flame and bring to a boil. Remove from fire. About 15 minutes before serving, place the fish escalopes in the nearly boiling sauce and poach until done. Meanwhile, slice the pimentos into julienne strips. Thinly slice the remaining fennel and sauté in butter for 1 minute. To serve, make a pool of sauce on each heated plate. Place the fish escalope in the centre. Carefully arrange the sliced, sautéed fennel on the fish and with the pimento julienne make a criss-cross pattern. Sprinkle chives around the edge of the plate on the sauce. Place the dish under a grill and heat. Serve immediately.

Serves 4

Roast Leg of Lamb Marinade

The Intrepids chef serves this with rice pilaf with rosemary, honey glazed carrots and courgettes with tarragon

1 leg of lamb about 1½ kg (3 lb)
3 tablespoons sugar
10 cloves garlic
60 ml (¼ cup) sherry
3 tablespoons vinegar
1 teaspoon pepper
2 tablespoons fresh chopped rosemary
1 tablespoon fresh chopped sage
4 tablespoons tomato paste

Place leg in a large bowl. Combine remaining ingredients and pour over the meat, turning well. Allow to marinate in a fridge overnight, turning occasionally. Roast or grill as usual.

Serves 6-8

Pear and Ginger Tart

Can be assembled and baked at last minute

1 22.5-cm (9 inch) uncooked pie crust
4 fresh pears, peeled, halved and cored
1 piece cinnamon bark
250 g (1 cup) sugar for poaching
200 g (¾ cup) sugar for syrup
1 teaspoon freshly grated ginger

Pre-heat oven (Gas Mark 5, 190°C, 375°F) and bake the piece crust half way. Poach the pears in a syrup made from sugar and 250 ml (1 cup) water and cinnamon bark. Cool, slice and arrange attractively over the pie shell. Make a sugar syrup from sugar and ½ cup water and cook to soft ball stage. (Test by dropping liquid into a cup half filled with cold water. Syrup should form a ball in your fingers.) Add the freshly grated ginger and quickly pour over the pears in the tart. Bake in a moderate oven (Gas Mark 5, 190°C, 375°F) until the shell is golden brown and the edges of the tart have begun to caramelise. Delicious with cream of any sort.

Serves 6

Chander Gupta Mauriya was a great Hindu king who reigned in the golden era of Indian history before the overthrow by the Mughals. The Nairobi restaurant named in his honour is a large, discreetly decorated room, with comfortable chairs and imported silver cutlery. Good music and great conversation are virtually guaranteed at the Mauriya, which features a menu of unusual dishes from different regions in India. The menu was launched by two chefs from the Taj Hotel in New Delhi, who prepare Mughlai, Peshwari and Hyderabadi dishes for a very discerning clientele. There are few more welcoming places than the Mauriya, where visitors are greeted like old friends and treated like royalty.

Murg Salai Kebab   spicy marinated chicken kebab

Prawns Taka-tak   ''taka-tak'' describes the sound made when this dish cooks

Achari Mutton   tender lamb in a spicy yoghurt sauce

Murg Salai Kebab

Salai means "needle", and needles, like this dish, should be handled with care

500 g (1 lb) boneless chicken, white meat
½ teaspoon red chilli powder
½ teaspoon garam masala powder (see Guide to Ingredients)
2 green chillies
1 teaspoon garlic and ginger paste (mix crushed garlic and crushed ginger in equal quantities)
2 tablespoons cashew nuts, ground into a fine powder
50 g (2 tablespoons) rendered mutton fat
salt to taste
75 g (½ cup) coriander (dhania) leaves

Mix all ingredients in a bowl and pass through a meat mincer twice. Shape around skewers in the form of sausages and grill over charcoal. Before serving, drizzle with melted butter and serve garnished with sliced onions, lemon wedges, sliced cucumbers and tomatoes. Mint chutney makes the ideal dip.

Serves 2

Prawns Taka-Tak

Use the freshest prawns you can buy for this delicious dish

1 tablespoon butter
1 onion, chopped
1 green pepper, chopped
4 green chillies, finely chopped
1 1-inch piece ginger, crushed
1 teaspoon ajwain (an Indian spice available in specialty stores)
2 tomatoes, peeled and chopped

Melt butter on an iron griddle or frying pan. Add chopped onion, green pepper, chillies, ginger and ajwain and fry 2-3 minutes over high heat. Add ginger-garlic paste and chopped tomatoes and sauté until masala is well cooked and the butter separates. Use a flat spatula to keep turning the mixture to avoid burning. Add prawns, salt, garam masala powder and fenugreek powder. Cook a further 3-4 minutes, constantly rotating the prawns with two flat spatulas. Add lemon juice and chopped fresh coriander. Serve in a flat dish garnished with onion rings and lemon

1 teaspoon ginger-garlic paste (use half quantities each of crushed ginger and crushed garlic)
500 g (8 oz) shelled queen prawns
salt to taste
¼ teaspoon fenugreek powder
¼ teaspoon garam masala (see Guide to Ingredients)
1 teaspoon lemon juice
chopped coriander leaves for garnish

wedges. Sprinkle coriander leaves on top. This can be served as a starter or as a main dish.

Serves 2

Achari Mutton
Taken from the kitchen of the Nawab of Hyderabad

500 g (1 lb) boneless lean lamb or mutton, in 1 inch cubes
500 ml (2 cups) natural yoghurt
2 large onions, sliced
salt to taste
1 teaspoon coriander powder
4 tablespoons oil
3 or more green chillies (according to taste)
60 g (2 tablespoons) mustard seeds
60 g (2 tablespoons) cumin seeds
10 g (1 teaspoon) onion seeds
10 g (1 teaspoon) fenugreek seeds
flour and water to make a stiff paste

Mix meat, yoghurt, onions, salt, coriander and oil in a pot. Fry over high heat until liquid is rendered from the meat. Simmer 5-10 minutes. Lower heat and let meat simmer until nearly tender (about 1-1½ hours). Slit green chillies lengthwise. Remove seeds. Mix together mustard, cumin, onion and fenugreek seeds and stuff into chillies. Sprinkle remaining seeds over meat. Place chillies in pot to cook with meat. Make a paste by mixing flour and a little water. Use paste to seal the lid of the cooking vessel. Place in a hot oven (Gas Mark 8, 250°C, 450°F) for 20 minutes. Serve hot.

Serves 3

Mount Kenya Safari Club

Food is an important component of the mystique of the Mount Kenya Safari Club, once the hideaway of the rich and famous. Now anyone can visit the club, optimally located for a perfect view of the craggy mountain which lures thousands of ambitious climbers up its slopes every year. Lunch is generally taken on the terrace overlooking the manicured grounds, where peacocks strut in the crisp, clear air. In the evenings, meals are served in one of two dining rooms—members have their own, rather more elegantly appointed space. Usually, the fare is interesting and plentiful, leaving you in the mood for a quiet evening by the fire, or a leisurely brandy in the bar.

Poached Fresh Fillet of Nile Perch Dugrele   a melange of fish in a flavourful wine sauce

Banana Mousse Mount Kenya   a deliciously cool dessert flavoured with Grand Marnier

Parfait Glacée Grand Marnier   a delicate frozen dessert

Poached Fresh Fillet of Nile Perch Dugrele

Serve with buttered broccoli and parsley potatoes

6 fillets of fresh Nile perch
500 ml (2 cups) white wine
1 bay leaf
1 small onion, chopped
½ teaspoon peppercorns
500 ml (2 cups) cream
6 shrimps, cleaned and cooked
12 mussels, cleaned and cooked
salt and pepper to taste
chopped parsley

Bring 1½ litres (6 cups) of water to boil with wine, bay leaf, onion and peppercorns in a deep sided frying pan. Lower heat, add fillets and poach until done. Remove fillets and keep warm in a low oven. Strain the broth and in a saucepan bring it to a boil with cream. Season and simmer for 20-25 minutes. To serve place a fillet on each plate, top with sauce and garnish with mussels and shrimp. Sprinkle with chopped parsley.

Serves 6

Banana Mousse Mount Kenya

Quick and easy

500 g (1 lb) peeled ripe bananas
250 g (1 cup) sugar
60 ml (¼ cup) Grand Marnier
500 ml (2 cups) fresh whipped cream

Liquidise the bananas in a blender or food processor. Place in a large bowl with sugar and mix thoroughly. Add Grand Marnier. Fold in whipped cream. Spoon into serving dish(es) and decorate with thin slivers of banana and a dollop of whipped cream. Refrigerate until served.

Serves 6

Parfait Glacée Grand Marnier
Prepare the day before serving

5 whole eggs, beaten
10 egg yolks, beaten
400 g (1½ cups) sugar
125 ml (½ cup) Grand Marnier
1 litre (4 cups) fresh whipped cream
glacé cherries for garnish
chocolate shavings for garnish

Whisk whole eggs, egg yolks, sugar and Grand Marnier until creamy on a very low heat. Remove from heat and allow to cool. Fold in whipped cream. Spoon into parfait glasses. Freeze for 24 hours. Garnish with shaved chocolate, glacé cherries and a dollop of whipped cream.

Serves 8

There are few more idyllic places for a restaurant than the white sands fringing the Indian Ocean on Mombasa's north coast. The Mvita Grill is best on a moonlit night with its view of the shimmery sea, bathed in a mysterious silver glow. Inside, there is a live band and careful attentive waiters, who will urge you to try the delicious seafood specialities prepared by chef Francis Sabwa, whose creativity is known and respected far beyond the Nyali Beach Hotel. He concentrates on perfect preparation of the dishes, as well as on original presentation of the food, some of the finest at the coast.

Avocado Ngomeni   flaked oysters in aspic

Mushrooms Mwambao   mushrooms and prawns flavoured with dhania, white wine and cheese

Sabwa's Mango Parfait   ice cream with mango sauce and Ivory Cream

Avocado Ngomeni
Garnish this lavish starter with whipped cream and caviar

1 dozen oysters
juice of ½ lemon
1 clove garlic, crushed
½ teaspoon salt
225 ml (1 cup) ready-made aspic jelly
45 ml (3 tablespoons) white wine
1 avocado, halved
salt and pepper to taste
2 teaspoons whipped unsweetened cream
1 teaspoon grated coconut
1 teaspoon caviar or Danish roe

Scrub oysters well under cold running water. Bring to a boil in a pot of water seasoned with lemon juice, crushed garlic and salt. Lift out of water, remove from shells, and add to liquid aspic. Add white wine and allow to cool for 1 hour. Flake jellied oysters using a fork. Fill avocado halves with aspic mixture. Place on a bed of shredded lettuce and garnish with whipped cream, coconut and caviar.

Serves 2

Mushrooms Mwambao
Good with or without the prawns

12 large mushrooms
2 tablespoons oil
2 tablespoons butter
225 g (8 oz) prawns, peeled (optional)
2 tomatoes, skinned, seeded and chopped
2 cloves garlic, crushed
1/3 cup chopped coriander leaves (dhania)

Wash mushrooms and remove stems. In a frying pan heat the oil. Add mushrooms and cook for 5 minutes. Remove from heat and put aside. Using the same pan, heat butter and add prawns, tomatoes, garlic, dhania, herbs, lemon juice and white wine. Cook over moderate heat for 5 minutes. Add cream and seasonings. Put mushrooms in hot serving dish and top with the sauce. Sprinkle with cheese and bake for 3 minutes (Gas Mark 6, 200°C, 400°F). Serve immediately.

mixed herbs to season
juice of 1 lemon
90 ml (1/3 cup) white wine
20 ml (1½ tablespoons) cream
pinch of white pepper
pinch of black pepper
pinch of cayenne pepper
25 g (2 tablespoons) grated cheddar cheese

Serves 4

Sabwa's Mango Parfait
You can substitute Bailey's Irish Cream for Ivory Cream

2 ripe mangoes
90 ml (1/3 cup) Ivory Cream
4 scoops vanilla ice cream
4 tablespoons caramelised cashew nuts

Place flesh of mango in a blender. Add Ivory Cream and blend until smooth. Put one scoop of ice cream in a tall glass. Pour mango sauce on top and sprinkle with caramelised cashews.

Serves 4

Nomad is the place south coast hotel keepers go to "get away from it all". Populated primarily by locals and "domestic tourists" from up-country, Nomad is the favoured hang-out for Kenya cowboys, their mothers, grandmothers, girlfriends, relatives from overseas and anyone else who can squeeze into the open-air restaurant. Anne and John Humphries are in charge of the food now, bringing Anne's own particular style to the original menu. Formerly of the Isaak Walton Hotel, and most recently managers of Seafarers, the Humphries are well known and well loved by all those of us who like good food served with a sense of humour.

Chilled Smoked Sailfish Soup   creamy and unique

Anne's Fresh Mango Chutney   zingy and fun as an accompaniment to just about any boring dish

Secret Lime Chicken   a recipe Anne said she would never reveal

Octopus Curry   an exotic seafood curry

Hot Passion·   just what the lady says

Banana Rum Pancake   zillions of calories in this super dessert

Chilled Smoked Sailfish Soup

Fresh dill is essential for this unbelievably delicious and original Humphries' soup

250-500g (8 oz to 1 lb) sliced smoked
   sailfish, or less if desired
2 medium onions, chopped
2-3 tablespoons chopped fresh drill
1 litre (4 cups) unsweetened yoghurt
1 litre (4 cups) milk
salt and crushed black pepper to taste
6 slices of lime
6 sprigs of fresh dill

Place smoked sailfish, onions and dill in a blender. Process until almost a paste. Add yoghurt slowly until blender is half full. Pour into a large glass bowl. Add remaining yoghurt, milk and a pinch of black pepper. Add salt to taste. Chill. Serve in chilled bowls with a slice of lime and a sprig of dill. This soup can be made 2 days before serving if refrigerated.

Serves 6

Anne's Fresh Mango Chutney

Anne explains that she "felt the recipe in my head, went on remote control and this is the result!"

3-4 mangoes, not quite ripe
1½ cups corn oil
1 tablespoon crushed garlic
1 tablespoon crushed fresh ginger
100 g (3 tablespoons) fish masala, or fish
   spices (see Guide to Ingredients)
1 heaped teaspoon sugar
3 teaspoons salt (or less)
2-3 cups inexpensive vinegar

Wash mangoes thoroughly. With a sharp knife, cut the flesh off the seed, leaving skin on. Dice in 2 cm (¾ inch) cubes. Put aside. Put oil in a heavy pan on low heat. Add garlic, ginger and spices all at once, stirring rapidly to prevent burning. Continue for 2 minutes, taking care not to burn. Add vinegar, sugar and salt. Boil very slowly for about 10 minutes, adding more vinegar if mixture appears to dry out. Remove from heat. Add mango cubes. Pour into jars, and refrigerate. Serve with cold meats, Indian meals, cheese or anything that wants spicing up.

Secret Lime Chicken

For the first time ever, Anne's secret weapon revealed!

6 spring chickens or 6 large pieces
½ bottle lime marmalade
3 tablespoons orange marmalade
1/3 jar mint sauce
4 bunches (2-3 tablespoons) chopped fresh coriander (dhania) (optional)
juice of 15 limes (or less if large and juicy)
375 ml (1½ cups) orange juice
salt to taste
sprigs of fresh coriander and mint for decoration

In a heavy saucepan, heat together the lime and orange marmalade, mint sauce, fresh chopped coriander, lime and orange juice. Boil for ½ minute, stirring with a wooden spoon. Remove from heat and add salt to taste. The sauce should have a sweet-sour taste. If too sweet, add more lime juice. Set aside. Heat oil in a pan and fry chicken pieces until well done. When cooked and crisp, remove from pan. Dip chicken in the sauce, completely submerging it. Place chicken on six heated plates and serve with vegetables and French fried potatoes. Serve sauce, heated to warm, in a sauce boat. Editor's note: I added half the quantity of lime juice and it was delicious!

Serves 6

Octopus Curry

The smaller octopus is most flavourful and tender

1 small octopus
250 ml (1 cup) vegetable oil
6 large onions, peeled and sliced
1 heaped tablespoon crushed garlic
1 heaped tablespoon crushed ginger
2½ tablespoons coriander powder
1½ tablespoons cumin powder

Cut up the octopus into 1½ cm (½ inch) pieces, removing the beak and eyes. Heat the oil in a heavy saucepan and fry the onions until soft but not brown. Add garlic and ginger and cook gently stirring with a wooden spoon. After ½ minute add the coriander and cumin powder and garam masala. Stir vigorously taking care not to burn. Add octopus, sufficient water to cover, beef stock cubes, sugar and lime juice. Boil gently for at least ½ hour, checking regularly to see it does not stick to the bottom of

2 tablespoons garam masala
   or substitute 6 tablespoons curry
    powder for the last three items
2 beef stock cubes
1 tablespoon sugar
1 tablespoon lime juice
salt to taste
chopped fresh coriander

the pan. Add water when necessary. When tender season carefully with salt (octopus is naturally salty so use care), and add fresh coriander. Serve with rice or chapatis.

Serves 4-6

Hot Passion
One of the most popular desserts on Anne's menu

3 grenadillas (passion fruit)
1 tablespoon sugar
1 teaspoon cornflour
1 tablespoon cream
2 eggs
1 tablespoon butter
½ banana, mashed
1 tablespoon sugar
bougainvillea or other flowers
   for decoration

Remove juice and seeds from grenadillas. Place all in a blender and blend for a few seconds. Strain. Add 1 tablespoon sugar and thicken with cornflour. Add cream. Separate eggs. Beat whites in a bowl until fluffy, not dry. In a small omelette pan, melt butter and add egg whites. Stir yolks in a bowl and pour over whipped whites. Score across the centre of the omelette and pour grenadilla sauce and mashed banana over one side. Sprinkle with remaining sugar. Fold over on a hot plate and serve, decorated with flowers.

Serves 1

Banana Rum Pancake

You can make it even more fattening with vanilla ice cream on top!

6 crepes (see p. 32 or p. 49)
8 bananas
2 tablespoons butter
juice of 2 limes
2 tablespoons brown sugar
2 tots of rum
lemon or lime for garnish

Place crepes on a plate. Cover with foil and place in a warm oven, along with six dessert dishes. Peel and slice bananas into chunky pieces. Melt butter in a frying pan. Add bananas and lime juice. Sprinkle with brown sugar and cook 1 minute over low flame, tossing or stirring gently to prevent burning. Add 1 tot of rum and set alight. Remove from heat. Place a pancake on each of the hot plates. Put the banana mixture on one half of the crepe, reserving a little for garnish. Trickle rum on the empty half of the crepe. Fold over and spoon more banana on top of the crepe. Garnish with lemon or lime wedges.

Serves 6

Twenty years ago the Peponi Hotel started with eight beds and a very simple kitchen. Today there are still only 21 beds, but the hotel is world famous, especially for the superb seafood caught just outside the front door. You can easily stay for more than two weeks at the hotel without being served the same dish twice. The menu is derived from what has been caught that day, making use of delicious lobster and crab, as well as very tasty small rock oysters. Many of the hotel's well-travelled guests claim Peponi's crab is the best in the world. The following recipes are simple enough to prepare at home, though let's face it, it will never be quite as magnificent without the view of a cerulean sea lapping a silver beach beneath a cloudless sky.

Tomato Lime Marmalade   a zingy breakfast jam

Carrot Soup   pale orange and creamy

Jodari   an appetiser based on Japanese sashimi, or raw fish

Whole Baked Fish with Coconut Sauce   Swahili style fish

Fish Mama Rukiya   a traditional Lamu recipe best prepared in a clay pot

Tomato Lime Marmalade

The most commonly requested recipe from Peponi

1 kg (2 lb) ripe tomatoes, skinned
16 limes
1 kg (4 cups) sugar
200 ml (approx. 1 cup) water

Cut tomatoes into small pieces, saving seeds. Finely pare skin from limes and cut into thin strips. Squeeze juice from limes and put aside. Boil cut peel, sugar and water together for approximately 10 minutes. Skim off any foam or scum which rises. (If you wish, you can place lime seeds in a muslin bag and boil with the mixture. This will slightly thicken the marmalade.) Add tomatoes and boil for a further 45 minutes or until mixture has reached the desired consistency. Add lime juice and boil an additional 10 minutes. (Editor's Note: Kenyan limes tend to be small. If using especially large or juicy limes use fewer than required number.)

Carrot Soup

Garnish with a dollop of sour cream and chopped parsley

25 g (2 tablespoons) butter
750 g (1½ lb) carrots, chopped
75 g (¾ cup) chopped onions
250 ml (1 cup) water
approximately 125 ml (½ cup) milk
1 teaspoon sugar
salt and pepper to taste

Melt butter in a large saucepan. Sauté carrots and onions for approximately 5 minutes, or until onions are tender and golden. Add water and simmer for ¾ hour. Add milk until desired consistency is achieved. Add sugar and salt and pepper to taste.

Serves 4

Jodari

The key to success of this delicacy is impeccable presentation

1 fresh tuna fish fillet
1 tablespoon soy sauce
1 teaspoon horseradish sauce or paste
1 lime

Slice the fillet very thinly across the grain. Arrange on a serving dish and chill. Make a sauce by mixing together ½ teaspoon horseradish with soy sauce and a few drops of lime juice. Stir well and serve in a tiny dish next to sliced fish. Keep the remaining horseradish separate and place on serving dish with wedges of lime.

Serves 4

Whole Baked Fish with Coconut Sauce

If fresh coconut is unavailable, use desiccated coconut to make coconut cream

1-2 kg (2-4 lb) whole cleaned fish
1 tablespoon butter
1 tablespoon lime pickle
2 cloves garlic, crushed
1 medium onion, sliced
1 tomato, skinned and sliced
salt and pepper to taste
juice of 2 limes
15 g (1 tablespoon) butter
100 g (1 cup) finely chopped onions
6 cloves garlic, crushed

Butter a baking dish large enough to hold the fish. Score the fish and place a few knobs of butter on top. Spread ½ tablespoon lime pickle over skin. Put remaining ½ tablespoon inside. Sprinkle crushed garlic over, distributing evenly. Slice onion and tomato and arrange on top of the fish. Sprinkle with salt and pepper. Pour lime juice over all. Cover the tray with tin foil and bake for approximately ½ hour in a moderate oven (Gas Mark 4, 180°C, 350°F). Make a sauce by melting butter in a frying pan and sautéing onion and garlic till soft. Add tomatoes and curry powder and fry for 4 minutes, stirring continuously. Add 1 tablespoon flour and half the thin coconut cream. Stir constantly. Add remaining flour and thin coconut cream. Simmer gently until thickened. Soak

2 fresh tomatoes, peeled and chopped
1 tablespoon curry powder
50 g (6 tablespoons) flour
2 cups thin coconut cream (see Guide to
   Ingredients)
50 g tamarind (see Guide to Ingredients)
125 ml (½ cup) water
½ cup thick coconut cream

tamarind in ½ cup hot water for 5 minutes. Squeeze softened tamarind in water to make a thick juice and add to sauce. Bring to a boil again, then switch off heat and add thick coconut cream. Do not allow to boil again. Season to taste with salt and pepper and serve with rice.

Serves 6

Fish Mama Rukiya

Mangoes give this dish an exotic flavour

1 kg (2 lb) fish fillets
1 large onion, chopped
3 medium tomatoes, peeled and sliced
5 cloves garlic, crushed
1 teaspoon black pepper
1 teaspoon turmeric
½ teaspoon onion juice
125 ml (½ cup) thin coconut cream (see
   Guide to Ingredients)
3 unripe mangoes, sliced
250 ml (1 cup) thick coconut cream

Butter a baking dish large enough to hold fish fillets and arrange them in layers with chopped onions and sliced tomatoes. Make a paste from the garlic, black pepper, turmeric and onion juice. Add ½ cup thin coconut cream and mix well. Pour remaining thin coconut cream over fish. Arrange sliced mangoes on fish and cover with thin coconut cream sauce. Bake in moderate oven (Gas Mark 4,180°C, 350°F) until fish is done and liquid evaporated, approximately 20-30 minutes. Pour thick coconut cream into baking dish. Return to oven and simmer gently for no more than 5 minutes more. The sauce should be creamy. Add salt to taste.

Serves 6

Rasoi

When we can't choose between Indian and Chinese fare, we go to Rasoi, a large, dimly lit restaurant opposite Nairobi's Professional Centre. With a lengthy menu of both types of cuisine, the restaurant provides enough choice for even the fussiest member of the family. Chinese food tends to be of the Szechuan variety, spicy and interesting, while the Indian food is light and well prepared. Five Indian chefs were brought to launch the restaurant, which serves an outstanding lunchtime buffet and an a la carte evening menu. We have included a selection of distinctive Indian and Chinese food in this section. Although it may seem strange, it is possible to mix the cultures, giving your guests an intriguing culinary experience.

Chicken Hot and Sour Soup   my favourite soup in Kenya

Prawns in Hot Garlic Sauce a highly distinctive starter or main course

Shahi Murg Malai   boneless chicken marinated in spices, cream and cheese

Manchurian Chicken   chillies liven up this superb chicken dish

Chicken Hot and Sour Soup

Spicy and hot, this soup is memorable

1 tablespoon oil
50 g (1/3 cup) shredded cabbage
50 g (¼ cup) finely chopped carrots
50 g (¼ cup) chopped radish
50 g (¼ cup) finely sliced bamboo shoots
500 ml (2 cups) chicken stock (can use chicken cube)
50 g (½ cup) beansprouts
100 g (3½ oz) chicken breast, cut into tiny pieces
salt and white pepper to taste
1 teaspoon vinegar
1 teaspoon soy sauce
pinch of monosodium glutamate (optional)
1½ tablespoons cornflour
1 egg, beaten
chopped spring onion to garnish

Heat oil in a saucepan. Stir-fry cabbage, carrots, radish and bamboo shoots for 3 minutes. Add chicken stock. Simmer for 3 minutes and add beansprouts, chicken, salt, pepper, vinegar, soy sauce and monosodium glutamate. Boil for 2 minutes. Mix cornflour in a tablespoon of cold water. Add to boiling stock and stir until thickened. Finally, stir in beaten egg and boil until cooked. Garnish with chopped spring onion.

Serves 4

Prawns in Hot Garlic Sauce
Expensive, but utterly delicious

1 kg (2 lb) medium prawns, cleaned and
    peeled
pinch of salt
pinch of white pepper
pinch of monosodium glutamate (optional)
1 teaspoon soy sauce
2 eggs
100 g (¾ cup) cornflour
oil for deep frying
½ teaspoon crushed ginger
½ teaspoon crushed garlic
100 g (1 cup) finely chopped red onions
50 g (½ cup) finely chopped green bell
    peppers
60 ml (¼ cup) chicken stock
50 g (1½ tablespoons) tomato ketchup
1 tablespoon vinegar
cornflour to thicken stock
6 spring onions, chopped

Place peeled prawns in a bowl. In another little bowl, mix together salt, pepper, soy sauce and monosodium glutamate. Toss with prawns and allow to sit for ½ hour. Mix together eggs and cornflour to make a batter. Heat oil in a large saucepan. Dip prawns in batter and deep fry. Put aside. Heat 2 tablespoons oil in a frying pan and add ginger, garlic, onions and green peppers. Add prawns and enough stock to moisten. Allow to simmer. Add tomato ketchup and vinegar and adjust seasoning. Let simmer again until well blended. Mix cornflour with rest of stock and pour into liquid. Boil until just thickened. Add chopped spring onions for garnish.

Serves 4

Shahi Murg Malai
Cheddar cheese and lemon juice add an indefineable flavour to this starter

2 chickens, de-boned and cut into portions
½ teaspoon salt
½ tablespoon red chilli powder
½ tablespoon garam masala (see Guide to
   Ingredients)
juice of 2 lemons
a paste of 1 tablespoon crushed ginger and
   1 tablespoon crushed garlic
100 g (¾ cup) grated cheddar cheese
375 ml (1½ cups) double cream
1 or more tablespoons chopped green
   chillies
lettuce

Place chicken pieces in a large bowl and cover with mixture of salt, chilli powder, garam masala, lemon juice and garlic-ginger paste. Grate cheese and add to chicken pieces. Pour cream over all and add chopped green chillies. Allow to marinate for 12-14 hours. Place chicken pieces on a barbecue and grill until cooked through. Serve on a bed of lettuce with condiments.

Serves 8

Manchurian Chicken
Have all ingredients ready for last minute preparation

4 boned chicken breasts
pinch of salt
pinch of white pepper
4 tablespoons soy sauce
pinch of monosodium glutamate (optional)

Place chicken pieces in a bowl. Mix together salt, white pepper, monosodium glutamate and soy sauce and pour over chicken. Allow to marinate for at least 1 hour. Reserve marinade for use later. Make a batter from flour, water and egg. Dip chicken in batter. Heat oil in a large frying pan and deep-fry the chicken till just done. Put aside. In a

½ cup cornflour
1 egg
¾ cup water
1½ teaspoons freshly chopped ginger
1½ teaspoons freshly crushed garlic
100 g (1 cup) finely chopped onion
1 teaspoon (or less) finely chopped green
  chilli
2 spring onions
185 ml (¾ cup) chicken stock
1 tablespoon tomato ketchup
1 tablespoon vinegar
1 tablespoon cornflour in 2 tablespoons
  water
oil for frying

saucepan heat a tablespoon of oil and fry chopped ginger, garlic, onions and green chillies until soft. Add chicken and spring onions. Add chicken stock and simmer. Add reserved marinade and adjust seasonings. Add ketchup and vinegar. Simmer until flavours are well blended, about 3 minutes. Add cornflour and water mixture and stir until thickened. More chicken stock may be added if necessary.

Serves 4

Rickshaw

The man behind the Rickshaw represents the second generation of Chinese restaurateurs to open in Nairobi. Richard Law, son of the Hong Kong Restaurant Law family has created a sophisticated setting for outstanding Chinese cuisine. Dim lights illuminate the interior of the restaurant, which is divided into private areas for intimate meals. To select a few specialities of the house from Richard's imaginative menu is to eliminate a host of dishes which have delighted his diners since the day the restaurant opened. In keeping with contemporary trends in the world, the food is light and very tasty, prepared on the spot by Chinese chefs who make it all look absurdly easy. You can achieve a reasonable facsimile at home...though without the flair which comes from years of continuous practice.

Stir-fried Chicken and Celery   a gentle main dish

Beef Fillet in Tangy Orange Sauce   easy, last-minute fare

Rickshaw Prawns   deep fried chilli-spiced prawns

Egg Fried Rice   the perfect accompaniment

Stir-fried Chicken and Celery

Use high heat to stir-fry chicken quickly

150 g (1 cup) shredded chicken
a few dashes soy sauce
salt to taste
1 teaspoon sugar
150 g (6 oz) celery, strings removed and cut
　diagonally
500 ml (2 cups) oil
2 cloves garlic, crushed
1 teaspoon cornflour
300 ml (1¼ cups) chicken stock
white pepper and salt to taste
½ teaspoon sugar

Place chicken in a small bowl and toss with soy sauce, salt and sugar. Allow to rest for ½ hour. Bring 2 cups of water to a boil in a saucepan. Drop in celery and boil for ½ minute. Drain and put aside. Heat oil in a wok or large heavy-bottomed saucepan. Quickly deep fry chicken for 1 minute. Drain. Remove oil, leaving only 2 tablespoons. Stir-fry chicken, adding celery and garlic, for 1 minute. Dissolve cornflour in ¼ cup chicken stock. Add cornflour mixture and remaining ingredients to the pan and heat until thickened, stirring all the time. Serve immediately in a heated dish with boiled rice.

Serves 4

Beef Fillet in Tangy Orange Sauce

Use the best quality beef for tender results

350 g (14 oz) beef fillet
½ teaspoon salt
½ teaspoon sugar
½ teaspoon white pepper
1 tablespoon oil

Cut fillet of beef into thin slices across the grain. Mix together next six ingredients and pour over beef. Allow to marinate at least 1 hour. Heat 2 tablespoons oil in a large frying pan. Stir-fry fillet until just cooked. Place cornflour in a cup. Add orange juice, sugar and salt. Add to pan and cook until thickened (about a minute). Serve with steamed rice.

½ teaspoon soy sauce
1 tablespoon cornflour
2 tablespoons oil
½ tablespoon cornflour
100 ml (1/3 cup) orange juice
¼ teaspoon sugar
¼ teaspoon salt

Serves 4

Rickshaw Prawns

A refreshingly easy, but very special way to prepare prawns of any size

300 g (10 oz) prawns
500 ml (2½ cups) oil
salt to taste
1 teaspoon sugar
2 cloves garlic, chopped
1 green chilli, finely chopped

Slit prawns along the back removing vein, keeping shells attached. Heat oil in a wok or large saucepan to appropriate temperature for deep frying. Fry prawns for 1 minute. Drain oil but leave oily. Mix remaining ingredients and add with prawns to wok. Stir-fry for another minute or two, until the prawns are done.

Serves 4

Egg Fried Rice

Serve as a welcome change from ordinary boiled rice

2-3 tablespoons oil
4 cups boiled white rice
2 eggs, beaten
1 spring onion, chopped
½ teaspoon salt
3 dashes soy sauce
pinch of pepper
pinch of sugar
90 ml (1/3 cup) chicken stock

Heat oil in a wok or large saucepan. Add boiled rice and stir-fry until cooked, over moderate heat. Push rice to one side and pour in egg, scrambling quickly. Mix rice and egg together and stir in seasonings, except for chicken stock. Finally, add chicken stock and serve.

Serves 4

I refuse to visit the north coast without stopping in to see Dolly Watts and Roy Macharia at the Seahaven, one of the friendliest and most appealing restaurants in Kenya. Visiting Roy and Dolly is like visiting your favourite relatives, the kind who won't let you leave without a taste of something fresh out of the oven. Their hospitality is legendary, and their cooking is what you wish your mother used to make. Seafood is the speciality at the Seahaven. Almost everything is decorated with flowers. Brilliant Bougainvillea, sweet smelling Frangipane, and delicate Flamboyant flowers set off the glorious lobster, prawn and crab dishes which arrive in the beautiful garden overlooking the Indian Ocean. Meals are long and leisurely affairs, with lots of wine or beer, endless conversation and far too much food. Getting recipes from Dolly is like pulling teeth. She never measures, has only a grater and a hand-mixer as kitchen equipment, and varies her dishes according to her moods ... the mark of a great cook!

Dolly's Deep Fried Prawns   butterfly prawns

Lobster Mwamba   lobster in its shell with wine sauce

Peanut Coconut Mould   a moulded caramel and ice cream dessert

Dolly's Deep-fried Prawns
An unforgettable hors d'oeuvre

8 queen prawns
1 egg
salt and pepper to taste
juice of 1 lime
60 g (½ cup) fresh breadcrumbs
oil for deep frying
125 ml (½ cup) mayonnaise
1 tablespoon ketchup
dash of Worcestershire sauce
dash of Tabasco
lime juice to taste
salt
1 teaspoon finely chopped parsley
1 teaspoon finely chopped onion
1 tablespoon finely chopped tomato
1 clove garlic, crushed

Peel and de-vein prawns, leaving the tails on. In a small bowl, beat egg together with salt, pepper and lime juice. Dip prawns in one at a time, and roll in fresh breadcrumbs. Heat oil in a saucepan. Deep fry prawns until golden brown. In a small bowl, mix together remaining ingredients to make a sauce. To serve, place sauce in a large brandy glass. Hang prawns over the side, tails out. Garnish with parsley and lemon or lime wedges.

Serves 2

Lobster Mwamba
A delicious alternative to Lobster Thermidor

1 lobster (500 g or 1¼ lb)
15 g (1 tablespoon) butter
1 onion, finely chopped
½ green pepper, finely chopped

Split the lobster down the back and remove the flesh. Place the shell in a large pan of boiling water and boil until shell is pink, about 10 minutes. Put aside to fill later. Cut lobster flesh into chunks. Fry onion, green pepper, mushrooms and garlic in butter until soft and golden. Carefully

5 button mushrooms, finely chopped
1 clove garlic, crushed
1 tablespoon flour
125 ml (½ cup) white wine
dash of Worcestershire sauce
250 ml (1 cup) single cream
salt and pepper to taste

add flour and cook for 1 minute stirring constantly. Add Worcestershire sauce and wine. Stir until sauce is well blended and thickened. Add lobster chunks and cook over a low heat until lobster is white and firm. Stir in cream and cook until heated through. Correct seasoning. Replace in lobster shell and gratinée until golden brown and bubbly. Serve accompanied by rice.

Serves 1-2

Peanut Coconut Mould

Can be prepared as a topping for ice cream as well

2 tablespoons peanut butter, softened
2 tablespoons freshly grated coconut
4 tablespoons sweetened condensed milk
2 portions vanilla ice cream

Mix first three ingredients together to make a rich sauce. Stir into ice cream and pack into a mould. Freeze.

Serves 2

Chilled to perfection, the Restaurant Shehnai offers Mombasa diners a sophisticated experience in Indian cuisine. The food is just right for the steamy coast: light, delicately flavoured Mughlai fare, cooked to perfection by a chef transplanted from Delhi. Manager Mr Zulfikan Harunani is an experienced and gracious host, who will recommend appropriate dishes for palates unaccustomed to the gentle spices of the Mughal Emperors, as well as the right choice for such dignitaries as the Prince of Bahrain, and Indian actor/director Manmohan Krishna, who are fans of his fine cuisine. The dishes selected here may look challenging, but are not impossible to reproduce accurately.

Subzi Kebab — grilled vegetable dumplings flavoured with coriander, chilli and turmeric

Reshmi Kebab — minced chicken kebabs rolled in cream

Ghosht Bhuna — tender mutton in a spicy yoghurt sauce

Shahi Firni — Indian rice pudding garnished with almonds and pistaccios

Subzi Kebab
A vegetable kebab makes an unusual starter

500 g (1 lb) potatoes
500 g (1 lb) green peas
1 large bunch spinach
1 large carrot, shredded
1 bunch coriander leaves (dhania), chopped finely
½ teaspoon chilli powder
½ teaspoon turmeric powder
½ teaspoon salt
2 tablespoons gram flour

Wash and boil the potatoes until tender. Peel and mash until soft. Boil spinach and green peas until tender. Add with remaining ingredients to potatoes and mash together. Mould vegetable mixture on to skewers. Grill over very low charcoal heat, slowly turning until golden brown. Remove from skewers and cut into pieces. Serve immediately on a bed of fresh salad with a slice of lemon and a dollop of hot chilli chutney.

Serves 4

Reshmi Kebab
Children particularly love the delicate flavours of this Shehnai speciality

2 kg (4 lb) chicken
1 bunch coriander leaves (dhania), chopped
½ teaspoon chilli powder
½ teaspoon salt
2 tablespoons fresh cream
4 tablespoons oil spiced with ½ teaspoon chilli powder

Remove the skins from chicken and carefully de-bone. Wash pieces thoroughly and mince finely in a food processor. In a large bowl, mix coriander leaves with chilli powder and salt. Add chicken and mix well. Leave for ½ hour for flavours to develop. Mould chicken mixture on skewers and grill over low charcoal heat until golden brown and cooked throughout. Remove from skewers and put aside. Heat spicy oil in a frying pan with the fresh cream. Add chicken kebabs and toss in the hot cream sauce for 3 minutes. Remove from heat and serve on a bed of finely chopped lettuce. Serve with lemon slices and chilli chutney.

Serves 4-6

Ghosht Bhuna

This meat lovers' delight originated from northern India

750 g (1½ lb) mutton, cubed
2 teaspoons crushed garlic
2 teaspoons crushed ginger
100 g (½ cup) ghee (see Guide to
    Ingredients)
150 g (1½ cups) chopped onions
2 cardamom pods
6 cloves
1 teaspoon cumin seeds
1 teaspoon black peppercorns
½ teaspoon chilli powder
½ teaspoon turmeric
125 ml (½ cup) yoghurt
150 g (5 oz) tomatoes, skinned, seeded and
    chopped
250 ml (1 cup) water
2 teaspoons salt
chopped fresh coriander

Make a paste by grinding the garlic and ginger together and set aside. Heat ghee in a frying pan and add onions, cardamom, cloves, cumin and peppercorns. When onion is tender and golden add chilli powder, turmeric and garlic/ginger paste. Stir over low heat for 1 minute. Next, slowly add the yoghurt, stirring all the time. Add tomatoes and cubed mutton and cook over moderate heat stirring constantly for 2 minutes. Add water and salt and simmer covered for 1½ hours or until mutton is tender. Serve in an oval dish, topped with chopped fresh coriander and accompanied by white rice.

Serves 4

Shahi Firni

Cardamom, almonds and pistaccio flavour this delicate rice pudding

80 g (½ cup) rice, cleaned
1.5 litres (2½ pints or 6 cups) whole milk
170 g (¾ cup) sugar
15 g (½ oz) cardamom pods, crushed
25 g (2 tablespoons) shredded almonds
25 g (2 tablespoons) shredded pistaccio nuts
¼ teaspoon saffron dissolved in ¼ cup water

Soak the rice in a large bowl of water for 1 hour. Drain and place in liquidiser with small amount of water. Grind to fine consistency. Place rice paste in a large saucepan. Add milk and cook over medium heat until creamy (about 25 minutes). And sugar and crushed cardamom pods. Stir gently over heat until sugar dissolves (5-10 minutes). Add half the shredded nuts and 6-8 drops of saffron water. Cool mixture and pour into small cups. Decorate with remaining almonds and pistaccios. Serve chilled or at room temperature.

Serves 4

The Stavrose has gone up-market, expanding from the slightly dingy, but very comfortable ground-floor premises on Nairobi's Banda Street to the glossy new surroundings of Post Bank House. The food has gone upmarket too, no longer featuring the simple, but utterly delicious favourites of the old days. The decor is charming, with a huge mural with a glittering mirror moon by artist Nani Croze, and lovely mirror-flecked, stained glass lamps to reflect the theme. Features such as outdoor seating and the salad cart make the Stavrose a popular luncheon choice. Everything contributes to a relaxed ambience which allows full appreciation of the fine cooking. Generous owner Kareem Karmali has shared his two most popular dishes.

Fish Goa   masala stuffed fish

Stavrose Mousse   a light, fluffy chocolate dessert

Fish Goa

Vary the chillies and cayenne pepper according to individual taste

tilapia fillets for four
1½-2 tablespoons chopped green chillies
   (according to taste)
5 teaspoons cayenne pepper (or less!)
2-3 tablespoons lemon juice
3 tablespoons white wine
3 tablespoons vinegar
pinch of salt
pinch of white pepper
flour for coating
oil for cooking
2 tablespoons white wine

In a small bowl, mix together the finely chopped green chillies, cayenne pepper, lemon juice, white wine, vinegar, salt and pepper to make a masala. Slit the tilapia fillets down the side leaving an inch on either side, making a pocket. Put the masala inside the pocket reserving 2 tablespoons for a sauce. Season the outside of the fish with more lemon juice, salt and pepper and coat in flour. Put cooking fat on a tray. Place under grill to heat. Place fish on hot tray and grill about 4 minutes each side, or until the fish is cooked. Remove fish to a heated platter. Heat remaining fat on the cooking pan. Add remaining masala. Thin with white wine and stir for 3-5 minutes or until the sauce thickens. Pour over the top of the fish and serve immediately on a plate decorated with lemon wedges, shredded lettuce, chopped parsley and sliced tomatoes.

Serves 4

Stavrose Mousse

A light version of a popular indulgence

4 eggs
4 teaspoons sugar
125 g (4 oz) cooking chocolate
1 tablespoon water

Separate the eggs. In a bowl beat the yolks with the sugar until smooth. Carefully, melt chocolate and water in a saucepan over boiling water. Add chocolate mixture to beaten eggs. Beat egg whites until stiff but not dry. Fold beaten whites into the egg yolk and chocolate mixture. Pour into a glass bowl or individual glasses and refrigerate to set for at least 2 hours. Garnish with whipped cream and shaved chocolate.

Serves 4

In Kenya, the name Tamarind is synonymous with good taste. The original Tamarind at the coast was joined by a Nairobi Tamarind, as well as a lively sister, the Carnivore, a haven for meat-eaters. Now there is the delightful Tamarind Dhow, anchored outside its namesake at the coast, which offers an exciting experience in open-air dining. The Tamarind managers are a dynamic and creative team, full of ideas which they support with tremendous hard work and commitment. The Tamarind recipes included here reflect the special quality that makes the group's restaurants so popular.

Crocodile in the Sky   a drink to make you see stars

Quail Egg Burgeret   smoked fish with quail eggs and caviar

Tamarind Bearnaise Sauce   good with meat, cooked vegetables or as a dip for marinated vegetables

Fillet of Fish with Camembert   fish on a clam shell

Passion Fruit Soufflé   a tangy delight

Crocodile in the Sky
A Tamarind house cocktail

6 tots (9 tablespoons) vodka
6 tots (9 tablespoons) orange liqueur
250 ml (1 cup) fresh passion fruit juice
3 tots (4½ tablespoons) fresh lime juice
1 tot (2½ tablespoons) sugar syrup
ice cubes
3 slices fresh orange, cut into halves
6 strawberries
sugar
1 lime

Put vodka, orange liqueur, passion juice, lime juice and sugar syrup into a jug over some ice cubes. Stir. Cut lime and rub the rims of six wine glasses with the edge. Dip the rims of the glasses into sugar and coat evenly. Put half an orange slice and a strawberry on a cocktail stick to use as a decoration for each drink. Strain the cocktail into the glasses and serve.

Serves 6

Quail Egg Burgeret
A sophisticated cocktail canapé

6 quails' eggs
6 round croutons 7-8 cm (3 inches) in diameter
280 g (10 oz) thinly sliced smoked trout or other smoked fish
6 tablespoons Bearnaise sauce (see following recipe)
3 teaspoons Danish caviar
6 sprigs of fresh dill

Toast croutons on both sides. Cover with smoked fish. Poach quails' eggs until yolk is soft (about 2 minutes). Do not allow to get cold. Spread 1 tablespoon Bearnaise sauce on the base of a small plate. Top with crouton. Place a poached egg on the crouton. Put half a teaspoon caviar on top of the egg. Decorate with a sprig of dill. Serve immediately.

Serves 6

Tamarind Bearnaise Sauce
A change from mayonnaise or Hollandaise sauce

5 tablespoons tarragon vinegar
3 sprigs fresh tarragon
3 sprigs chervil
1 tablespoon chopped onions or shallots
2 black peppercorns, crushed
4 egg yolks
15 ml (1 tablespoon) water
250 g (1 cup) softened unsalted butter
salt to taste
lemon or lime juice to taste
cayenne pepper

Boil vinegar, tarragon, chervil, onions and pepper until 3 tablespoons remain. Remove from heat. Beat egg yolks with the water in a bowl. Add vinegar mixture and pour into the top of a double boiler. Stir briskly over hot, but not boiling water until the sauce is light and fluffy. Add butter, a little at a time, stirring constantly. Add salt, cayenne and lime juice to taste. Sauce must be kept warm over a double boiler. Serve as soon as possible.

Makes 310 ml (1¼ cups)

Fillet of Fish with Camembert
Bake in a clam shell

300 g (10 oz) fresh fish fillets
juice of 1 lime
1 tablespoon grated Parmesan cheese
15 g (1 tablespoon) butter
2 small tomatoes, skinned and sliced
2 medium white onions, thinly sliced
1 gherkin, thinly sliced

Cut the fillets into 4-6 thin pieces. Rub lime juice over fillets. Sprinkle Parmesan on top. Butter an ovenproof dish. Place 2 clam shells in the dish and butter well. Put in the fish. Cover each with the onion, tomato, gherkin and Camembert slices. Sprinkle dill, paprika, pepper and salt on top. In a small pan, melt the butter and add flour, mixing until smooth. Add wine and fish stock. Cook through, stirring continuously while heating to ensure mixture is smooth. Pour over fish. Cover dish with foil

125 g (4 oz) Camembert cheese, thinly
    sliced
1 teaspoon fresh dill
2 teaspoons paprika
½ teaspoon salt
freshly ground black pepper to taste
50 g (3 tablespoons) butter
1 tablespoon flour
125 ml (½ cup) white wine
125 ml (½ cup) fish stock

and bake in a hot oven (Gas Mark 6, 200°C, 400°F) for 15-20 minutes or until sauce is bubbly. Serve with buttered rice.

Serves 2

Passion Fruit Soufflé
With a hint of orange liqueur

7 eggs, separated
180 g (¾ cup) sugar
500 ml (2 cups) passion fruit juice
2 tots (3 tablespoons) orange liqueur
4 rounded tablespoons gelatine
7 tablespoons lime juice
300 ml (1¼ cups) double cream
chopped toasted nuts

Beat egg yolks and sugar in a heavy bowl over hot water. Remove from the heat and continue beating until cold. Fold in the passion juice carefully. Fold in the orange liqueur. Spoon gelatine over lime juice in a glass bowl. Leave until spongy. Stand bowl in hot water until ALL the gelatine has dissolved. Cool and stir into the passion mixture. Whip cream until thick and fold into the passion mixture. Beat egg whites until stiff and fold into the mixture. Spoon into a 7 inch souffle dish which has been prepared in advance. Cover with waxed paper. Chill until set. Take the paper off the bowl before serving and decorate side of souffle with chopped nuts.

The New Stanley Hotel is a Nairobi landmark. Robert Ruark and Ernest Hemingway were regulars in the good old days, and no doubt picked up inspiration for some of their tales from the great white hunters who used to frequent the bar. These days the clientele is almost equally divided between tourists and locals, with most of the action outside in the Thorn Tree Cafe, under the shade of the most famous thorn tree in Kenya. Upstairs, the atmosphere is more refined, with a quiet residents' lounge and the Tate Room, where the food reflects an inventive use of local ingredients.

Bouillabaisse Mombasa Style   African version of a French classic

Trout Naro Moro   bananas and green peppers are an unusual accompaniment to fresh trout

Coupe Mount Kenya   ice cream with coffee liqueur and strawberries

Florentine Kilifi   honeyed cashew nuts, cherries and currants on a pastry shell base

Bouillabaisse Mombasa Style
A meal in itself

2 kg (4 lb) assorted fish and seafood such as
 red snapper fillets, kingfish fillets, cut
 into 3 inch pieces
600 g (1¼ lb) lobster and prawns, cleaned
 and shells removed, cut into bite-size
 pieces
125 g (1¼ cups) chopped onion
100 g (4 oz) tomatoes, peeled and sliced
4 cloves garlic, crushed
1 piece of dried orange peel
1 branch fennel
2 sprigs parsley
2 sprigs thyme
1 bay leaf
100 ml (1/3 cup) olive oil
1 pinch saffron
salt and freshly ground black pepper

Prepare fish fillets and shell fish. Place vegetables and herbs in a large saucepan. Cover with lobster, prawns and firm-fleshed fish. Sprinkle with olive oil and saffron, season with salt and freshly ground pepper. Cover with water. Bring to boil and simmer for 7-8 minutes. Add delicate fish. Continue boiling for another 7-8 minutes or until all the fish is perfectly cooked but not mushy. Serve garnished with parsley accompanied by chunks of warm French bread.

Serves 6

Trout Naro Moro
Serve with fluffy white rice and tossed salad

2 kg (4 lb) fresh trout
50 ml (1/5 cup) Worcestershire sauce
juice of 1 lemon
salt and pepper
flour for dusting fish
80 g (5 tablespoons) salted butter
150 g (5 oz) banana slices
150 g (1½ cups) chopped green pepper
175 ml (¾ cup) fish stock
1 whole lemon
watercress

Place trout fillets in a large pan. Mix together Worcestershire sauce, lemon juice, salt and pepper and pour over fillets. Allow to marinate for 1 hour or more. Remove trout and dust with flour. Clarify butter by heating until foamy, then pour off butter, leaving particles in the pan. Pour clarified butter into a large frying pan, heat and fry fish until browned on both sides. Remove from pan and place on a serving dish to keep hot. Pour off most of the butter and gently fry bananas and pepper slices until soft. Add fish stock and bring to a boil, stirring continuously. Pour over fish and garnish with lemon wedges and watercress.

Serves 10

Coupe Mount Kenya
Substitute Kahlua or any coffee liqueur for a popular dessert

¼ cup fresh pineapple chunks
a few strawberries
2 tablespoons Mount Kenya liqueur
3 scoops vanilla ice cream
60 g (¼ cup) whipped cream
chopped roasted cashew nuts for garnish

Marinate pineapple and strawberries in liqueur. Place two scoops of ice cream in a tall glass. Pour over marinated fruits. Top with another scoop and more fruit. Pipe whipped cream over the ice cream and sprinkle with cashew nuts if desired.

Serves 1

Florentine Kilifi
Quite simply the most delicious Florentine I know

250 g (2 cups) flour
150 g (¾ cup) unsalted butter
125 g (1 cup) icing sugar
2 egg yolks
1 tablespoon milk
250 ml (1 cup) single cream
300 g (1¼ cups) unsalted butter
500 g (1½ cups) granulated sugar
200 g (¾ cup) honey
600 g (4½ cups) cashew nuts, chopped
300 g (2 cups) glace cherries
200 g (1¼ cups) currants

In a large mixing bowl, cream together soft butter with sugar. Add eggs and mix until light and fluffy. Stir in flour and milk and beat until well mixed. Dough should be stiff. Add flour as necessary. Place in fridge for at least 1 hour. When well chilled, roll out to fit a large baking tin (40cm x 30 cm, or 16 inches by 12 inches). Place in hot oven (Gas Mark 8, 280°C, 450°F) till half cooked, about 20 minutes. To make filling, warm butter and cream in a large saucepan until butter is melted. Add sugar and honey and cook until soft ball stage. (Test for soft ball by placing a small amount of syrup in a cup of hot water. It should form a soft ball you can pick up in your fingers.) In a large bowl, mix together cashew nuts, currants and chopped cherries. Pour hot mixture into bowl and mix well. Allow to cool slightly. Pour over half-baked pastry crust and bake in hot oven as before until golden brown. If possible, allow to cool for 12 hours and cut into squares.
(Editors Note: You will appreciate the quantity the recipe provides more fully after you have tasted them. They also freeze well.)

Makes 30-40 squares

You won't find a more unlikely location for a Yugoslav restaurant than the grimy Adam's Arcade Shopping Centre. But tucked away behind bamboo curtains is Wilco, one of the town's most industrious cooks. Although he has worked as executive chef in several of the country's finest hotels, he is happiest when he rolls up his sleeves and prepares the Balkan food which has made his little restaurant famous. The food is ideally suited to Kenyan ingredients and lifestyle; much of the meat is barbecued at the last minute, and garnished with vinegary salads, coleslaw with rye and lovely sauteed potatoes.

Ajvar   spicy cold barbecue sauce

Gravce Tavce   Yugoslavian bean stew

Cevapcici   Balkan "nyama choma" or grilled meat kebabs

Balkan Goulash   the "curry" of eastern Europe

Ajvar

Excellent for spicing up any grilled meat

500 g (1 lb) red bell peppers
250 g (8 oz) carrots, cut in half lengthwise
2 tomatoes
2 teaspoons crushed garlic
3 tablespoons vinegar
salt, pepper and chillies to taste
5 tablespoons oil

Wash the peppers and carrots and place in an oven until they become limp and the skins are shrivelled. Cut the peppers in half and remove the seeds and stem. Peel the carrots. Place in a mincer or food processor with the tomatoes and crushed garlic, and mince. Add the vinegar and seasonings. Place all in a pot and boil until it thickens, about 10 minutes. Remove from fire. Allow to cool and whisk in the oil. The sauce should have a bright red colour and be thick enough not to run off a spoon.

Serves 10

Gravce Tavce

Meat or potatoes may be added if desired

500 g (1 lb) dry red or brown beans
60 ml (¼ cup) oil
1½ onions, chopped
2 teaspoons crushed garlic
3 teaspoons paprika powder
½ teaspoon ground black pepper
1 teaspoon tomato paste

Soak the beans in cold water for several hours. Boil in fresh salted water until tender but not overcooked (skins should be intact). Cut the tomato and pepper into 2 cm (¾ inch) pieces. In a saucepan fry the onions in oil until golden brown. Remove from heat and add garlic and seasonings while still hot. Add beans and remaining ingredients and boil for an additional 10-15 minutes adding more stock if necessary. Serve with chunks of fresh bread and grilled meat.

1 teaspoon salt
¼ teaspoon chopped chilli (optional)
1 teaspoon chopped parsley
2 tomatoes
1 green pepper
500 ml (2 cups) beef or chicken stock

Serves 8-10

Cevapcici

For best results use the leanest meat possible

700 g (1½ lb) minced (ground) beef
300 g (10 oz) minced (ground) pork or
   lamb
1½ teaspoons crushed garlic
1½ teaspoons crushed black pepper
4 tablespoons cold water
salt to taste

Mix all ingredients thoroughly by hand and refrigerate for 1-2 hours. Remove and mix again. Roll into finger-length sausages. Brush well with oil. Cover with greaseproof paper and return to the refrigerator for another hour to allow the oil to tenderise the meat. Grill over a moderate charcoal fire until golden brown and juicy. Serve with onion rings, fried potatoes, salad and Ajvar.

Serves 6

Balkan Goulash

Left-over Goulash can be eaten as the Yugoslavs do — reheated for breakfast with fresh bread

1 kg (2 lb) beef shin or topside
4 heaped teaspoons paprika
3 teaspoons salt
125 ml (½ cup) oil
1½ heaped teaspoons marjoram
1½ teaspoons carraway seeds
½ heaped teaspoon crushed peppercorns
1½ heaped teaspoons crushed garlic
½ teaspoon chopped chilli
1 fresh tomato, chopped
500 g (1 lb) white onions, sliced
2 heaped teaspoons tomato paste

Cut meat into 2 cm (¾ inch) cubes. Place in a bowl and mix with salt and half the paprika. Set aside for 15 minutes. In a large saucepan heat the oil and fry the garlic and spices over moderate heat taking care not to burn. Add cubed meat, chopped onions, tomato and tomato paste. Braise first over high heat stirring occasionally to keep from burning. When juices are nearly reduced add stock or water and simmer until the meat is cooked. Add liquid as necessary to maintain gravy. The gravy should take on a reddish brown colour, onions should be completely dissolved and gravy should be thick enough to cling to meat. Serve with mashed or boiled potatoes, noodles or rice.

Serves 4-5

All recipes have been written with a choice of continental gram and litre measurements or American cups. Select one and stay with it for the best results.

Chillies: be careful when cutting fresh chillies and never rub your eyes when handling them. Store chillies in the refrigerator as they lose their flavour quickly.

Coconut milk: to prepare thick coconut milk place one cup of water and one cup chopped coconut flesh in a blender. Blend at high speed until coconut is reduced to a smooth purée. To make in the traditional method, pour one cup hot water over one cup grated coconut flesh (or use unsweetened desiccated coconut). Use fingers to squeeze coconut to extract juices and oils. Ideally, let mixture stand for up to 2 hours. Strain. To make thin coconut milk, repeat the procedure with the same coconut. The resulting milk will be thinner and less rich.

Coriander: (also called dhania or cilantro) is available in speciality shops in the United States and England. Buy coriander in bunches and keep fresh by refrigerating until needed.

Garam Masala or Masala: the Indian term for curry powder. In Kenya we are fortunate in having an extensive selection of masalas provided by Indian ration or spice shops. However, when unable to obtain the specific masala required substitute any other good curry powder.

Garlic: cloves tend to be small in Kenya averaging 2 medium cloves to one teaspoon. If using larger cloves adjust recipes accordingly.

Ghee: clarified butter, commonly used in Indian cooking. Unlike butter it can be kept for months in a hot climate. Substitute any other cooking fat if not available.

Ginger root: many of the recipes in the book call for fresh ginger root or stem. Peel the root before chopping. If not available, substitute half the quantity of fresh ground ginger.

Hollandaise Sauce:
125 g (½ cup) butter
1½ tablespoons lemon juice
3 egg yolks
1 tablespoon boiling water
3 tablespoons water
¼ teaspoon salt
dash of cayenne pepper
Melt butter is a small pan. Put aside. Heat lemon juice until just warm. Beat egg yolks in top of a double boiler until they begin to thicken. Stir in 1 tablespoon boiling water and beat. Continue beating, while adding the remaining water. Beat in lemon juice. Remove double boiler from the heat and continue beating while adding the melted butter in a slow stream. Season with salt and cayenne.

Limes: in Kenya limes are more common than lemons and tend to be much smaller than those in the United States. Adjust the number of limes required accordingly.

Tamarind: a brown pod grown in the tropics containing a number of seeds embedded in an aromatic sweet-acrid pulp that is used in chutneys, syrups for juices and sauces (Worcestershire). Lemon juice of citric acid may be used as a substitute in a smaller quantity.

White sauce: melt 30 g (2 tablespoons) butter or margarine in a pan. Stir in 30 g (¼ cup) flour. Slowly add 250 ml (1 cup) milk and stir over low heat until thick. Season with salt and white pepper.

Aberdare Country Club, Nyeri. Tel. Mweiga 17/25
Akasaka, 680 Hotel, Standard Street, Nairobi. Tel. 20299
Alan Bobbe's Bistro, Caltex House, Koinange Street, Nairobi. Tel. 21152, 26027, 24945
Amboseli Grill, Hilton Hotel, Mama Ngina Street, Nairobi. Tel. 334000
The Bay Leaf Caterers, P.O. Box 20104, Nairobi. Tel. 767432, 762906
China Plate, Accra Road, Nairobi. Tel. 20900, 25225
El Patio, Reinsurance Plaza, Taifa Street, Nairobi. Tel. 340114
Foresta Magnetica, Corner House, Mama Ngina Street, Nairobi. Tel. 23662
Ibis Grill, Norfolk Hotel, Harry Thuku Road, Nairobi. Tel. 335422
Imani Dhow, Severin Sea Lodge, Mombasa. Tel. 485001, 485212
Island Camp, Lake Baringo. Tel. (Nairobi) 25641, 25941
Jax Restaurant, Kimathi Street, Nairobi. Tel. 28365, 23427
Khyber, Meridian Court Hotel, Muranga Road, Nairobi. Tel. 339956, 331365
La Galleria & The Toona Tree, International Casino, Nairobi. Tel. 742600
Le Chevalier, Muthaiga Shopping Centre, Limuru Road, Nairobi. Tel. 748269
Maharaja Hotel, Muindi Mbingu Street, Nairobi. Tel. 27880
Makaa Grill, Jadini Beach Hotel, Diani. Tel. 2052, 2149
Mara Intrepids, Masai Mara Game Reserve. Tel. (Nairobi) 335208, 338568
Mauriya, Manohar Centre, Westlands, Nairobi. Tel. 747691, 747695
Mount Kenya Safari Club, Nanyuki. Tel. 2141/2
Mvita Grill, Nyali Beach Hotel, Mombasa. Tel. 471551
Nomad Restaurant & Beach Bar, Diani. Tel. 2155
Peponi Hotel, Lamu. Tel. 3029
Rasoi, Parliament Road, Nairobi. Tel. 25082, 26049
Rickshaw, Fedha Towers, Kaunda Street, Nairobi. Tel. 23604
Seahaven, Mombasa. Tel. 485351
Shehnai Restaurant, Mungano Street, Mombasa. Tel. 312492

Stavrose, Post Bank House, Banda Street, Nairobi. Tel. 335107
Tamarind Nairobi, Harambee Avenue. Tel. 338959
Tamarind Mombasa, Nyali. Tel. 471747, 472263
Tate Room, New Stanley Hotel, Kimathi Street, Nairobi. Tel. 333233
Taurus, Adam's Arcade, Nairobi. Tel. 567696
Trattoria, Wabera Street, Nairobi. Tel. 340855